The Answer to

STRESS

Resting in Him

Mary Ann Kiszla

By

Mary Ann Kiszla

Published by

In Him Publishing
18004 Sun Ridge Circle
Noblesville, Indiana 46060
317/867-1260

In Him Publishing
18004 Sun Ridge Circle
Noblesville, Indiana 46060

ISBN: 0-9650415-6-5

Second Printing 2001

To my Father and His Son
Who called me to rest in Them.
What a difference it makes
as I do.

FOREWORD

It's exciting to learn something new. It's even more exciting to put it into practice and see   it work. You may find a better way of doing something on the computer. Yesterday an expert walked me through a new program. My first reaction was "I didn't know you   could do that." Or you may make a profound discovery that changes your life. And you say, "I didn't know you could live that way." Suddenly your eyes are open to new possibilities. They've been around for a long time, but you just found out about them. You want to share these new insights with others so they can benefit too.

Several years ago the Lord began teaching me about the greatest stress reliever in the world. That's what this book is all about.

It's not just another quick fix to tide you over until something better comes along. It works and keeps on working. If you're under a lot of stress, you need this reliever. And even if you aren't stressed out at the present moment, you still need it. Circumstances can change quickly and problems pop up where you least expect them. So press on. I pray by the time you finish reading this book, you can't wait to try it yourself. You'll be glad you did. It will change your life.

TABLE OF CONTENTS

Chapter

IT'S AN EXCITING LIFE

You have made known to me
The paths of life;
You will fill me with joy
in your presence.

Acts 2:28

IT'S AN EXCITING LIFE

One of the most penetrating lessons I've ever learned is to rest in the Lord. The impact on my life has been tremendous. My perspective has changed. How I look at things and react to them is decidedly different.

It all began two years ago when my husband and I went on a fall retreat. Our purpose was to get away with the Lord for a few days. We simply wanted to spend more time with Him and get to know Him better without all the interruptions and distractions at home. We planned to delve into the Word and prayer more deeply. There were no deadlines. There was no pressure. Our time was His time. And we thought: "Wouldn't it be great if it were like this at home!"

Shortly before our departure, the Lord put it on my heart to write a word study on resting in Him. With Bible and concordance in hand, I diligently searched the Scriptures for relevant references. As I wrote, I saw how much God loved His people, how deeply He cared for them. He wanted them to rely on Him alone. On the Sabbath, He called them to rest from their work and to focus on Him instead. It was a day to remember who He was and whose they were and to appreciate all He had done for them. He was their God and they were His people. We took the word study with us. The subject of resting in Him turned out to be of prime importance on our retreat. The more we studied about it, the more excited we became. Resting wasn't just for them. It was for us too. We decided to try it.

What an awesome teacher God is. He's tender yet tough. Patient but persistent. He's training us for life. He wants us to be prepared. There's so much to learn, it takes a lifetime to grasp it. Some lessons are extremely difficult and don't sink in immediately. We have to go over them again and again until they finally take hold and become a part of us. But God doesn't give up. He knows head knowledge isn't enough. It doesn't stick with us, but quickly slips away. His lessons must penetrate our hearts before we can live them.

As Hank and I began to live this way, we found that everything comes together in Him. It's not what we try to do for God that matters, it's what He does through us. Rather than doing things our way, we yielded to His. It's the difference between self reliance and relying on Him. The Lord told Paul: "My grace is sufficient for you, for my power is made perfect in weakness." [1] This holds true for us today.

How has resting affected us? For one thing, we've seen its effect on the stress in our lives. That's something most of us can't escape. Different things cause pressure and anxiety in people. What paralyzes one may not faze another. What seems trivial and insignificant to you may be of paramount importance to someone else. We are diverse, yet we all seem to have our share of stress.

But resting has to do with much more than stress. It affects every area of our lives. As Hank and I began to rest in the Lord, we drew closer to Him and got to know Him better. There's a contentment. Calmness, assurance and joy permeate our lives. We don't strain to live the way we know we should. We've learned trying harder and harder doesn't help us become what He wants us to be. Yielding to Him does. We're aware of what we have in Him and appreciate Him more. In our work, we no longer carry the entire load ourselves because we're yoked with the Master. Teamed up with Him. And we have the greatest resources in the world available to us. His.

Experts in business have told us in order to make a go of our ministry, we need the three w's. Wealth, wisdom, and work. Those who have the money or know where to get it. Those with the expertise or brains. And those who are willing to do the work. But we discovered we already have all that in the Lord. His wealth is unlimited. He is omniscient. And He does the work.

Does this mean we sit back and do nothing? No. We follow His leading instead of going off on our own. When we rest in the Lord, we do what He calls us to do in His power and strength, not ours. The results are far better and there's an absence of stress and strain.

Are all problems eliminated? Adversities still come, but instead of panic, there's peace in the middle of them. We don't ignore the situations that confront us. We're very aware of what the consequences may

---

[1] 2 Corinthians 12:9

be. But instead of trying to solve the problems ourselves, we turn to Him with them. "How are we going to handle this one, Lord?" We don't have the answer, but He does.

Be forewarned. This way of life does not come naturally. It's not something you grew up with or learned in school. The world continually tells us: "Stand on your own two feet. You can do whatever you put your mind to if you just try hard enough. If you want something done right, you'd better do it yourself." It's self effort right down the line.

Trust in the Lord with all your heart and lean not on your own understanding,[2] does not compute with most of us. It goes against the grain. If you want to live this way, you need to make a deliberate decision to do so every day. You choose to rest in Him moment by moment. The longer you live this way, the more it becomes a part of you. And you find you're resting in Him without even thinking about it.

Who is this rest for? You. The Lord knows what's going on in your life. He knows your hopes and dreams as well as your fears and frustrations. He wants to be your shelter from the storms that come along and ravage your life. You can find this rest in Him alone. He wants this for each of us.

Why should you try it? What's in it for you? It's the answer to the stress in your life. There's peace instead. The zingers will still come, but you'll react to them differently. If the roof caves in, you won't. When you're resting in the Lord, He handles the problems. He's there in the middle of the adversities and helps you through them. It's exciting to see Him at work. Every day is one of anticipation and expectation. You look forward to it. With Him, you have it all!

Read on to find out more about this life in Him. He doesn't want you to miss it.

---

[2] Proverbs 3:5

To Think About:

Do you want to get closer to the Lord and know Him better?

How do you think this will change your life?

Prayer

How loving You are, Father. Thank you for drawing me closer and teaching me to rest in You. You want this even more than I do. Help me to let go of the distractions and keep my eyes on You instead. What peace and contentment there is when I do. Thank you for Jesus who made it all possible. It's in His name I pray.

CHAPTER 2

IN GOD ALONE

*My soul finds rest
in God alone;*

Psalm 62:1

IN GOD ALONE

For many of us, life moves along at a harried pace. We live in a stress-filled world and there's a great deal of uncertainty in our lives. We may not be able to change the circumstances, but we look for a release from it. An escape.

We often turn to people or things as diversions from the tension and pressure. Listening to good music gets our mind off the situation confronting us. Reading a good book soothes us. Calling family or friends helps. Or going to a movie. The list goes on and on. These are stop gaps at best. Temporary, but they don't last. When the CD has ended, we've finished the book, the conversation is over and we hang up the phone, or we exit the theater, stress once again invades our mind.

There is a better place where we can turn to relieve our anxiety, however; one that has longer lasting effects. Find rest, O my soul in God alone;...[1] The psalmist, David, did not have an easy life. His was filled with a great deal of stress. He often poured out his heart to the One he knew would listen. That was where he found the true rest he was seeking. He who dwells in the shelter of the Most High will rest in the shadow of the Almighty.[2] God was the refuge he turned to in his time of need.

Why is our rest in God alone? For one thing, He created us." You are worthy, our Lord and God, to receive glory and honor and power, for you created all things, and by your will they were created and have their being." [3] Who knows us better than He does? Who knows his creation better than the One who created it? He knows each of us by name and everything about us. With six billion people in the world, that is truly amazing. He's aware of our strengths and weaknesses. Our good points and bad. He even knows what we're thinking and feeling at any moment during the day. O Lord, you have searched me and you know me. You know when I sit and when I rise; you perceive my thoughts

---

[1] Psalm 62:5

[2] Psalm 91: 1.

[3] Revelation 4:11

from afar. You discern my going out and my lying down; you are familiar with all my ways. Before a word is on my tongue, you know it completely, O Lord.[4]

Recently I was shopping for linens for our guest bedroom. I had stopped at a discount store to pick up some incidentals before heading for the department store nearby. As I walked through the aisles, I thought about looking for sheets there. They would probably be less expensive and do just as well. As soon as that thought came to mind, the Lord spoke very clearly. "You will not get your sheets here." I turned around to see who had spoken. No one was in sight. Again He emphasized, "You will not get your sheets here."

I got the message, paid for my purchases and headed for the other store. Unknown to me, there was a huge sale going on there. I quickly found percale sheets, much better than I had intended to buy for far less than I would have paid at the first store. It's a bit disconcerting when the Lord stops you in mid- thought, but I've learned He knows what is best even when I don't.

Why is our rest in God alone? Not only were we created by Him but also for Him. We often overlook that aspect of our creation. We were made by God and for God. Designed by Him for Him. He put a need in each of us for Him alone. There's a void that only He can fill. No one else can do it. Many search for substitutes, but substitutes can never fully satisfy.

Then God said, "Let us make man in our image, in our likeness,.." [5] God created man so he could communicate with his Creator. He wants us close to Him. He wants to be an integral part of our life, at the very center of it. He's the One who makes our life complete. The intimacy Adam had with God before the fall, God's Son restored to us by His death on the cross.

---

[4] Psalm 139: 1-4
[5] Genesis 1:26

Jesus is the One who holds our life together... in him all things hold together.[6] When things are falling apart, He's the glue that keeps them together. We need Him. We can't do it on our own. He never intended for us to.

Sometimes when I'm restless and can't figure out why, I finally realize it's the Lord calling me to rest in Him. I may not be aware that I need rest, but He does. He knows I can't get along without it.

A recent study showed that a sleep deficit of merely a few hours each night had a tremendous effect on those participating in it. Instead of their usual eight hours, they slept one to three fewer hours. Over a period of time, this lack of sleep caught up with them. Those conducting the study found that the participants' bodies had actually aged a great deal and their performance was vastly affected. However, when they slept more hours than were needed each night, they returned to normal again. The extra sleep was able to turn back the clock. Remember when your mother used to warn: "You need your sleep. You can't burn the candle at both ends." She was right. We need to get sufficient rest every day. A worn out body doesn't perform well. The mind isn't as sharp. We slow down and it takes an enormous effort to get anything done. When we don't get enough sleep, we're irritable and don't function as efficiently.

Not only do our physical bodies need rest, but our souls need rest as well. A weary soul becomes dull and insensitive to God's leading. It is easily discouraged. Jesus calls to us, "Come to me. I'll give you rest." We are revived as we rest in Him. He encourages us and gives us hope.

Why is our rest found in God alone? Consider for a moment His great love for us, a love that never lets go. This is how God showed his love among us: He sent his one and only Son into the world that we might live through him.[7] He forgives us when we stubbornly go our own way, and then turn back to Him once more. How patiently He waits for our

---

[6] Colossians 1:17b
[7] I John 4:9

return. He welcomes us with open arms just as the father did his prodigal son. As we look at our Father's unfailing love, we know we can rest secure in Him. How great is the love the Father has lavished on us, that we should be called children of God! And that is what we are![8] What a privilege we have. He is our Father. We are His children. You may not have an earthly father who loves you, but you have a Heavenly One who does.

God has plans for each of us. "For I know the plans I have for you," declares the Lord, "plans to prosper you and not to harm you, plans to give you hope and a future." [9] He wants His very best for us. Only He can bring that about. He does as we trust Him and rest in Him.

Why is our rest in God alone? Why not in someone else? Our Father never changes. "I the Lord do not change." [10] Neither does His Son. Jesus Christ is the same yesterday and today and forever.[11] We don't have to wonder what God is going to be like today or what He will be like tomorrow. We already know. In this world where people and things change so quickly, it's good to know we can count on Him. People are fickle. Hot one minute, cold the next. Friendly one time, distant another. He is not. He always stays the same. He is compassionate, faithful, slow to anger, forgiving, abounding in love. Who wouldn't want to rest in Him?

I will lie down and sleep in peace, for you alone, O Lord, make me dwell in safety.[12] Each night, I crawl into His waiting arms and fall sound asleep. I rest content, knowing how very much He loves me. And I realize in Him, I have it all.

---

[8] I John 3:1

[9] Jeremiah 29:11

[10] Malachi 3:6

[11] Hebrews 13:8

[12] Psalm 4:8

To Think About:

Where do you look for rest?

Do you turn to the Lord when you're going through tough times?

Who knows you better than anyone else?

Who alone can fill all your needs?

Prayer

Father, my soul finds rest in You alone. Who knows me better than You do? There's a need in me that no one else can fill. You never change. I'm so grateful that I can always count on You. I come to You in the name of Your Son, Jesus, who holds everything together.

CHAPTER 3

WHAT DOES IT MEAN TO REST IN HIM?

The Lord is my shepherd, I shall not be in want.
He makes me lie down in green pastures,
he leads me beside quiet waters,
he restores my soul.

Psalm 23:1-3a

WHAT DOES IT MEAN TO REST IN HIM?

There is so much unrest in the world today. People frantically search for something better, but nothing seems to satisfy. Jobs don't. Wealth doesn't. Power is fleeting. If they have one thing, they yearn for another. They continually hope and constantly hunt for something more. Maybe that will be the answer and satiate their desires. Those in the market place who claw their way to the top often find it's a hollow victory. It doesn't satisfy either. Rather than fulfillment, they find emptiness instead.

Solomon, the wisest and wealthiest man on earth put it this way: "Utterly meaningless! Everything is meaningless." [1] God had greatly blessed this man. He had it all. Yet in his old age, Solomon turned from God to what he knew was wrong. In his quest for something new and different under the sun, he ran after people rather than seeking God. Ensnared by their ways, he began worshiping worthless idols instead of only the one true God. He had it all, but settled for far less. And he found it was meaningless.

How do you get rid of the restlessness in your life? Where can you find peace instead? By turning to the One who gives you rest. He's the only One who can. There is a need in each of us for Him - a void that only He can fill. Our Creator put it there.

In your quest for rest, start with Jesus. He loves you so much He was willing to die on a cross so you could have this rest in Him. He made peace with His Father for you by His blood that was poured out on the cross. We are all sinners and only His blood could cleanse us and wash us clean. God said there is no rest for the wicked. If we don't accept Jesus' gracious offer of forgiveness, we are still sinners caught up in our sins. But we can get rid of the sin and unrest in our lives by turning to Him. Nothing else works. That's the way our Father planned it.

What an example Jesus is to us. When He lived here on earth, He showed us how to rest. How often He turned to His Father for comfort and strength. Sometimes Jesus spent all night with Him. He needed that time of refreshing. But Jesus also rested in the Almighty One as He

---

[1] Ecclesiastes 1:2b

carried out His work. He said to His disciples: The words I say to you are not just my own. Rather, it is the Father, living in me, who is doing his work."[2]

Whenever I think about rest, my thoughts turn to the gentle Shepherd tending His sheep. The Lord is my shepherd, I shall not be in want. He makes me lie down in green pastures, he leads me beside quiet waters, he restores my soul.[3]

I'm one of His lambs. He calls me by name and leads me into a lush green meadow beside a quiet stream. It's so peaceful there. I know my Shepherd's voice and He knows mine. I eagerly follow wherever He leads me. I trust the Master with my life. How tenderly He cares for me, protects me and fills my needs. As I take time with the Good Shepherd, I am refreshed in His presence. Not only is my body at rest, but my soul and spirit are as well.

Jesus said: "Come to me, all you who are weary and burdened, and I will give you rest. Take my yoke upon you and learn from me, for I am gentle and humble in heart, and you will find rest for your souls. For my yoke is easy and my burden is light." [4] In this chaotic, harried world, I need time with the Shepherd every day. He doesn't want me struggling to achieve on my own. Instead He says, "Let me help you. Be yoked with me. Then the burden won't be so heavy."

Have you ever noticed how little children don't want their parents out of their sight? There's a security in knowing Mom and Dad are there. If they walk into another room, the little ones frantically search for them. "Mommy, Daddy where are you?" When asked, "what's wrong?", they answer, "Nothing. I just wanted to know where you were." That's the way we are with the Lord. We just want to know He's there.

Jesus tells us: "So do not worry, saying, 'What shall we eat?' or 'What shall we drink?' or 'What shall we wear?' For the pagans run after all these things, and your heavenly Father knows that you need them. But seek first his kingdom and his righteousness, and all these things will be given to you as well." [5]

---

[2] John 14:10b
[3] Psalm 23:1-3a
[4] Matthew 11:28-30
[5] Matthew 6:31-33

Our problem is we run after things instead of going to the One who fills those needs. We focus on getting instead of seeking Him. How often we fall into this snare. Our Father wants first place in our lives. He is well aware of our needs and will fulfill them, but He expects us to seek Him first. He says," Be still and know that I am God;" [6] He tells us, "Stop striving. Listen to Me instead. I am everything you need now or will ever need. In Me, you have it all."

What is rest? How would you define it? The first thing we usually think of is physical rest. We all need it. That's vital for our health. But our body can be at rest, while our mind is far from it. We may plop down in a recliner, prop up our feet but our anxious thoughts continually flit from one concern to another. It's much easier to quiet our body than our mind.

Resting in the Lord is more than merely resting our bodies, important as that is. It involves our total being, including our soul and spirit as well. *Resting in Him begins on the inside. It's an attitude of the heart. A way of life.*

What is resting in the Lord? Just that—resting in Him, yielding yourself totally to Him and letting Him be in charge. Trusting Him with your life. It's resting not only when you're sitting quietly with Him but also as you carry out His work. He who dwells in the shelter of the Most High will rest in the shadow of the Almighty.[7] God told Moses: "My presence will go with you, and I will give you rest.[8] *When you live in God's presence, you will be at rest. It doesn't matter where you are or what you are doing. He is there with you.*

When you rest in Him, you stop trying to do things yourself. You do them in His power and strength. Nothing you do on your own can compare with what He does. Self effort strains to live the way you know you should but keeps failing. Resting means releasing your life to Him every day and letting Him work His way in you. Trying harder and harder won't do it. You need His help.

---

[6] Psalm 46:10a
[7] Psalm 91:1
[8] Exodus 33:14

24

Suppose you're married with young children. One way says: "I am going to be the most loving person there is today. I am going to love my spouse and be patient with the kids no matter what." Think of the stress you're putting on yourself. Your intentions are admirable, but often they don't last long.

The other way says: "Lord, I need You. I want to be more loving to my spouse, but I'm having a hard time. And I want to be more patient with the kids but they're really getting to me. You are so loving and patient with me. Would You put your love in me for my spouse and give me Your patience for my children?"

One way leads to frustration. The other freedom. You don't have to be a super man or woman, just one who's surrendered to Him. That's they key. It's not enough to know what to do, you need His help to do it.

As you rest in the Lord, you no longer hinder Him or thwart His plans. You don't run ahead of Him or lag behind. You walk hand in hand with Him. You have everything to gain by resting in Him. How often we miss God's best for us because we miss Him.

Instead of worrying about the "what ifs" of tomorrow or "if onlys" of yesterday, you focus on today and live it to the fullest. That's all you really have. Today. Yesterday is over and done with and you don't know what tomorrow will bring. You know He can handle anything that comes along.

How will you know when you're resting in Him? Not only will you notice the change in your life, so will others. The strain is gone. A heavy load has been lifted off your shoulders. You're free. The stress that plagued you has been replaced with an indescribable peace. Joy fills your heart. You are content. Resting is a new way of life...one He highly recommends.

To Think About:

Is something missing in your life?

Do you take time with the Good Shepherd every day?

How does that help?

Prayer

What a difference You make in my life, Father. You freed me from the stress and strain and gave me peace instead. Thank you for Jesus, the Good Shepherd who watches over me and shows me the way. I come to You in His name.

CHAPTER 4

REASONS TO REST

*Peace I leave with you;
My peace I give you.*

John 14:27a

REASONS TO REST

Tell a little child to do something and the first thing he asks is, "Why?" Like little children, we sometimes wonder, "Why should I do that? What's in it for me?" Let's look at a few reasons why we should rest and the benefits we receive when we do.

First of all, *our Father tells us to.* He set the example. By the seventh day God had finished the work he had been doing; so on the seventh day he rested from all his work. And God blessed the seventh day and made it holy, because on it he rested from all the work of creating that he had done.[1] When God finished creating the heavens and the earth and everything in it, he rested. He took time to sit back and look at what He had made. He was finished. He had completed His creation and saw that it was good. He didn't rest because He was tired. He simply wanted to enjoy it. And He set apart that day as holy.

Our Father said we should rest from our work too. It's a special time for us to be with Him. For some of us, resting is hard to do. We're workaholics. We don't know when to quit. If we finish one project, there's a big letdown until we start another one. We're restless if there is nothing to do. We don't know how to relax. We aren't satisfied unless we're busy. But if we're working all the time, when do we have a chance to relish the rewards of our labor? More importantly, when do we find time for Him?

Jesus said: "Come to me, all you who are weary and burdened and I will give you rest."[2] The Master often sees us struggling and getting nowhere. Instead of trying to do things ourselves, He calls us to turn to Him for help. He's always accessible and He knows us better than we know ourselves. He's aware of when we're worn out and need rest.

Why rest? Because we need it. Mentally, physically, and spiritually. *Rest is good for our health.* We all need our rest. God created us that way. Miss one night's sleep and you won't function as well the next

---

[1] Genesis 2:2-3
[2] Matthew 11:28

morning. Your mind is in a fog. Miss several in a row and not only will you know it, but so will others. And when you consistently cut back on your time with the Lord, you will be spiritually depleted. You are short-changing yourself.

A time of rest gets us back on track with the Lord again. We take stock of where we are and the direction in which we're heading. Goals may need to be re-evaluated as we step back and look at the bigger picture. Are we where God wants us to be, doing what He calls us to do? If we charge ahead without conferring or consulting with Him, we may end up lost and off course. Far from where He intends us to be.

Why do we need to rest? *Because we're so busy.* You may think, "That doesn't make sense. I'm so busy I don't have time to rest even if I wanted to." That's when you need rest the most. The busier you are, the more you need to take periodic time outs. You can't afford not to. If you don't, burnout isn't far behind. In vain you rise early and stay up late, toiling for food to eat - for he grants sleep to those he loves.[3]

Answers to problems we've been wrestling with often come when we're resting. We aren't even thinking about them. Our minds are totally relaxed and open to God's solution. And we wonder, "Why didn't we think of that before?" Because we were so engrossed in the problem, we weren't receptive to the answer.

Why do we need to rest? *Resting in the Lord defeats the evil one.* One of Satan's most successful ploys is keeping us so busy we have no time left for the Lord. His strategy is to wear us out as we frantically rush from one thing to another. He doesn't want the Creator counseling us or exposing his schemes.

It pleases God greatly when we seek Him and take time to rest in Him. He wants us to draw near to Him. There are so many benefits when we do. We're refreshed from being in His presence. I can attest to what a difference He makes. He lifts my spirit. I may be tired or discouraged when I sit down with Him, but it isn't long before I am revived. What an encourager He is!

---

[3] Psalm 127:2

There's a contentment that comes from resting in Him. I look at what I have, not what I don't have. And I realize in Him, I have it all.

There's a joy that only He can give. 'You have made known to me the paths of life; you will fill me with joy in your presence.' [4] I'm smiling on the inside.

There's also a peace that comes from Him. Peace I leave with you; my peace I give you. I do not give to you as the world gives. Do not let your hearts be troubled and do not be afraid.[5] The world's peace is so fragile. It's easily broken. But I find God's peace lasts because it depends on Him, not circumstances or what's happening to me.

My hope in Him. As I contemplate what lies ahead, I am not afraid. He is my future. He knows precisely what is going to happen. He will be with me and see me through it. Find rest, O my soul, in God alone; my hope comes from him.[6]

And when I rest in Him, *I won't be shaken.* He wants me to be unflappable. I will be as I rest in Him. He is my refuge and haven, and the One who keeps me safe in the middle of life's storms. I am secure in Him.

When I rest in Him, I'm a different person. My outlook is changed, as well as my actions. Why rest in Him? Your life will never be the same if you do.

---

[4] Acts 2:28
[5] John 14:27
[6] Psalm 62:5

To Think About:

What would it take to convince you to rest in the Lord?

Are you willing to try it?

Prayer

I have every reason to rest in You, Father. Instead of
chaos, there's contentment. When I'm very busy, I need
You even more. I'm a different person when I rest in
You. Help me to remember that and do so every day.
Thank you for Your Son who set the example for me.
It's in His name I pray.

CHAPTER 5

HOW DO YOU BEGIN?

*Come near to God and
He will come near to you.*

James 4:8a

HOW DO YOU BEGIN?

How do you rest in the Lord? *It's a matter of the heart.* When you love someone, you want to be with him. You yearn to know him better. You want to have a intimate relationship with him. That's what our Heavenly Father desires for each of us. He wants us close to Him.

How do you begin? *You rest in His presence.* Come near to God and he will come near to you.[1] He wants this even more than you do. He's already waiting for you to take that first step. He never intended for you to live this life on your own. He knows you can't do it. He wants to be included in every part of it. The whole purpose of Jesus' coming to earth and dying on a cross was to reconcile us with our Father so we could have this close relationship with Him. Jesus said, "I am the way and the truth and the life. No one comes to the Father except through me." [2]

Some would rather keep God at a distance. They don't want to get close to Him. He's there in case they need Him. An option in their hip pocket. It's like car insurance. They hope they won't have an occasion to use it. They want only so much of God. A little goes a long way with them. If only they knew what they were missing.

Your Father loves you and wants to be with you. Not only now and then, but every single day. Even with six billion people in the world, He knows you by name. You're not just a number to Him. He knows everything about you. How precious you are to Him.

Not only does God know you personally, He wants you to know Him too. He went to so much trouble so you can. When Jesus was here on earth, He showed us what our Father is like. He said if you know Him, you will know the Father. They are one. Your Father desires to give you His very best. *It's all wrapped up in your relationship with Him. Out of that comes everything else.*

What does God expect from you? He wants you to love Him with all your heart. When you love Him wholeheartedly, you want to be with

---

[1] James 4:8a
[2] John 14:6

34

Him as much as possible. You make time for Him everyday. Instead of a burden, you consider it a privilege. Nothing can keep you away. You long to know Him better. You want more than mere facts about Him, you want to know Him personally. Nothing less is enough.

Resting is a matter of priorities. When you acknowledge He is the most important part of your life, you will seek Him. When you realize your time with Him is the most meaningful part of your day, you won't miss it. It doesn't matter how busy you are. In fact, the busier you are, the more you need Him. You don't want anything to crowd Him out. When you understand how vital your relationship with Him is, you will do everything possible to protect and nurture it. This relationship isn't stagnant. It's a continual process. In a state of flux. You're either growing closer to the Lord or slowly slipping away and you may not even know it.

Resting is a matter of choice. It's a decision you make. Are you tired of all the hassle, the stress and the strain in your life? Do you wonder if there's more to life than that? Are you ready and willing to do something about it? Then take time to rest in the Lord each day.

When is the best time to do it? Early morning with Him is a great way to begin the day. It's quieter then and distractions are fewer before the urgency of today hits. Each night I ask the Lord to awaken me early the next morning to spend precious time with Him. This prepares me for what lies ahead. He's the One who wakes me up, but it's my responsibility to get up. He does His part and He expects me to do mine. On those dark, cold mornings it takes a bit more effort.

Night time may be better for you. Instead of TV, turn to Him. If you have a family, you may have to wait until everyone else is in bed. Evenings can be busy seeing to their needs. As you rest in Him, you are preparing for the day ahead. When you end the day with Him, you sleep better.

A friend finds early afternoon is best for her, so she takes a few hours with the Lord then. *It doesn't matter when you make time for Him. The important thing is to do it.* Short breaks with Him during the day help too. At your job, you can even incorporate these with lunch or coffee breaks. They keep your focus on Him.

Write out a few of your favorite Scriptures on three by five cards. Tuck one or two in your wallet to carry with you. As you read them, they remind you of what you have in the Lord. We call these our "faith cards" and keep adding to them. Some are getting so dog-eared from use, we've had to rewrite them.

What if you miss a day or two in your time with the Lord? Start in again. Don't give up. Keep at it. When I know I'm going to be especially rushed in the days ahead, I try to take extra time with Him beforehand. That sees me through the busy periods.

How do you rest in Him? Seek Him out. He tells us: "You will seek me and find me when you seek me with all your heart.[3] Spend time with Him and get to know Him better. Love Him and appreciate Him. Let Him be a vital part of each day. Be aware of this tremendous privilege He's given you and thank Him for it. As you do, your life will never be the same. Life with Him is so much better.

What do you do when you rest in Him? Sometimes you just sit quietly with Him. He has your full attention. You don't have to say a word. He's aware of what you're thinking or feeling. When you love someone, you just want to be with him. You don't have to talk continually. Take time to listen to Him. Praise Him for who He is. Thank Him for making you His and for what He's doing in your life. Read His Word and ask Him to teach you. What does He want you to learn from it? Pray. Hand over your concerns to Him as well as those you have for others. He promises He'll watch over you and show you which way to go and He does.

Resting in Him is being aware of His presence all day long. It's leaning on the Lord rather than yourself as you go about your work. He's on the job with you. You do it in His power and strength. And whatever you have to do, it's done as unto Him. He's the One you're really serving. He's the One for whom you work. The simplest things become a pleasure because you want to please Him. You'll find you care a little more about your job. You want to do the very best you can. Sometimes He even shows you a better way of doing it. *Resting is walking hand in hand with the Master.* He's fully aware of what you face each day and He's there to help you through it. What better hands could you be in?

---

[3] Jeremiah 29:13

To Think About:

Would you like to rest in the Lord?

Then seek Him every day. He'll meet you where you are.

What can you do to get to know Him better?

Are you willing to do it?

Prayer

Resting is all wrapped up in my relationship with You, Father. That's where it all begins - with You. Thank you for taking time with me and meeting me where I am. I love You and   want to be with You. Help me to show my love by the way I live today. I come to You in the name of Jesus, the Reconciler.

IT'S A MATTER OF TRUST

I will say of the Lord,
"He is my refuge and my fortress,
my God in whom I trust."

Psalm 91:2

IT'S A MATTER OF TRUST

Think about the people you can relax with. Those you like to be around. People with whom you can just be yourself. Watch an expectant little child eagerly lift his hands to be picked up. Sometimes he's upset or irritable and doesn't even know why. He needs to be comforted or maybe he just wants to be loved. Once his mother takes him in her arms, draws him close and snuggles him, he relaxes and rests in the arms that encircle him. He soon drifts off to sleep. He's content to be with the one who loves him. He trusts her completely.

Likewise, if we are to rest in our Heavenly Father, we too must trust Him. Not only for what He will do for us, but more importantly for *who* He is. He is our Father and we are His children and He lavishes us with His love. Just as an earthly father loves his children and wants to be with them, so our Heavenly Father wants us near Him. He does whatever it takes ... even to the point of sending His Son to die on a cross.

Our Father created us for Himself. As His children, we often try His patience and break His heart, but He still loves us with a love that never lets go. He doesn't give up on us. Isn't that incredible! His love for us is so great, we can't begin to fathom it. *We simply need to accept it.* How that must grieve Him when we don't, when it's there for the taking. But when we do bask in His love, it's like warm sunshine that fills our souls.

If we don't trust Him, we can't rest in Him. We won't give ourselves to Him completely. Instead, we stubbornly cling to our way and miss His best for us. I wonder how often we do that and don't even realize it.

I've been reading through the Old Testament again. Each time I do, it sinks in a little deeper and I begin to see the bigger picture. What a future God had in mind for His people. What promises He gave them. Yet time after time they failed to trust Him. They saw first hand the many miracles He performed in Egypt. They were delivered from the throes of Pharaoh. Crossing the Red Sea on dry ground must have been awesome; something they would never forget. Only an Almighty God could have done that. But seeing those things didn't make believers out of them. It didn't draw them closer to God. They simply wanted more. They grumbled and complained. Nothing was ever enough. For forty years I was angry with that generation; I said, "They are a people whose hearts go astray, and they have not known my ways." So I declared on oath in my anger, "they shall never enter my rest." [1] And they didn't.

Trust and obedience go together. If we trust our Father, we will obey Him. Scripture calls it obedience that comes from faith. Where there is a lack of trust, rebellion results instead. How often the Israelites rebelled against God.

God said from now on you're going to have to live by faith and not by sight. Too often our motto has been: "Seeing is believing. Show me first, then I'll believe you." That isn't the way it works. He says: "Believe Me, then I will show you." Sometimes that's hard to do, especially when there's a significant lapse of time between believing and seeing. We're tempted to give up rather than trusting Him to come through no matter how long it takes. He tells us it's impossible to please Him without faith. Yet how often we try.

As I was thinking about this, the Lord kept impressing upon me that a little trust is no trust at all. Think about it. It's not a case of, "I trust You Lord, but..." and then we go on to enumerate why we can't. Or "I can trust You for this but not for that." We either trust Him or we don't. He isn't trustworthy in some things and not in others. That's like saying a part of Him is to be trusted, but not another. He is wholly trustworthy. *We're trusting in the character and reputation of God. We trust Him for who He is.* A pittance of trust only gets us part way there. Complete trust sees His promises fulfilled.

One morning recently, I asked the Lord what happens when I doubt. He showed me a clear, new light bulb that burned brightly and one that was dirty and emitted a very dim glow. What a contrast between the two. I am to be His light in the world. When I doubt, it's like a dusty, sticky film that encrusts my light and witness to others. It dulls it. If I am to be that light that burns brightly, I must keep my mind on Him. Doubt departs when I do.

As believers, we are to live by faith, not by sight. What is seen is only temporary. What is unseen is eternal. *I know that in my head, but sometimes my heart lags behind.* Even as I come to the Lord with my cares and concerns, I know He is already working them out. He knows what the solutions are. I don't, but He does.

---

[1] Psalm 95:10-11

God alone is trustworthy...worthy to be trusted. Yet how quick we are to trust others and how slow to put our faith in Him. It is better to take refuge in the Lord than to trust in man.[2] People often let us down. He never does. We can count on Him and depend on Him. Those who know your name will trust in you, for you, Lord, have never forsaken those who seek you.[3]

Our trust isn't merely in trusting, but rather in the One whom we trust. Sometimes, if I'm having trouble believing Him for something and my faith begins to waver a little, He asks, "Haven't I already proved Myself to you?" Thoughts of all He has done fill my mind and heart. Then I realize where my focus has been... not on Him, but on me. And I quickly shift my attention back to Him - all that He is and whose I am.

In Hebrews we read: See to it, brothers, that none of you has a sinful, unbelieving heart that turns away from the living God.[4] That's what happens when we doubt. Instead of moving toward Him, we move away from Him. *It's a step in the wrong direction.*

Think about the twelve men who spied out the Promised Land. Two were excited about what they found and were ready to take what God had promised them. Ten saw the good land, but were overwhelmed by the sight of giants who lived there. *Their faith fled in the face of fear.* They didn't trust God for what He said He would do. Instead of enjoying God's best, they perished in the wilderness. They never entered God's Promised Land.

Many of us put our trust elsewhere than in God. Wealth is our security. His reply? Whoever trusts in his riches will fall. [5] Or we look to other people and pin our hopes on them. This is what the Lord says: "Cursed is the one who trusts in man, who depends on flesh for his strength and whose heart turns away from the Lord." [6] Some look to themselves and their own abilities. He who trusts in himself is a fool.[7]

---

[2] Psalm 118:8
[3] Psalm 9:10
[4] Hebrews 3:12
[5] Proverbs 11:28
[6] Jeremiah 17:5
[7] Proverbs 28:26

Can you imagine how God must feel when we don't trust Him? When we realize who He is and all that He is, how can we *not* trust Him? If we can't trust God who created everything there is, whom can we trust?

Consider Moses confronting Pharaoh time after time and threatening him with disaster if he doesn't let God's people go. Or picture him at the edge of the Red Sea. Pharaoh's men are rapidly approaching and there is literally no where to go. No escape. There is only one place to turn. When God told Moses to raise his staff and stretch his hand over the sea, he didn't say, "I certainly hope you know what you're doing, God. There's a lot of water out there." He knew God would come through and take them across safely. He didn't know how, but He knew He would. He even told the Israelites who were intently watching everything that was going on: "Do not be afraid. Stand firm and you will see the deliverance the Lord will bring you today. The Egyptians you see today you will never see again. The Lord will fight for you; you need only to be still." [8] Moses said this before God did a thing. He trusted his Maker. And the people saw God's mighty power as He parted the Red Sea.

What about you? Do you trust God for You? Do you say, "God can do anything. Nothing is impossible for Him." That's true, but do you believe He *will*? *And do you believe He will do it for you?* The hardest person to believe God for is yourself. It's a lot easier to believe Him for someone else. Merely stating that God can do something is a safe answer. But when you say He will, you're climbing out on a limb. That's faith and we can't please God without it.

What happens when we trust Him? He who dwells in the shelter of the Most High will rest in the shadow of the Almighty. I will say of the Lord, "He is my refuge and my fortress, my God, in whom I trust." [9] When we trust Him, *we rest secure in Him* just like the little child in the arms of his mother.

There's a peace that comes when we trust our Father. It comes only from Him. Thou wilt keep him in perfect peace, whose mind is stayed on thee: because he trusteth in thee. [10] He alone can and will keep us in His perfect peace as our minds are fixed on Him. Why? Because we trust Him.

---

[8] Exodus 14:13-14
[9] Psalm 91:1-2
[10] Isaiah 26:3 KJ

Joy and thanksgiving well up within us. We can't stop praising Him and thanking Him. The Lord is my strength and my shield; my heart trusts in him, and I am helped. My heart leaps for joy and I will give thanks to him in song. [11] In him our hearts rejoice, for we trust in his holy name.[12]

When we trust Him, *we are blessed.* O Lord Almighty, blessed is the man who trusts in you.[13]

And when we trust Him, *we won't be shaken.* We're in His hands and nothing throws Him. He is unflappable. He is in control. Those who trust in the Lord are like Mount Zion, which cannot be shaken but endures forever.[14]

---

[11] Psalm 28:7
[12] Psalm 33:21
[13] Psalm 84:12
[14] Psalm 125:1

To Think About:

Read Psalm 31:14-15

Can you say, "Lord, I trust you with my life. My times are in Your hands."

If not, ask the Lord to show you what keeps you from doing so. Be willing to let go of it.

Jesus said: "Do not let your hearts be troubled. Trust in God; trust also in me." [15] Do you believe He means that for You?

Have you ever taken hold of one of God's promises only to see your faith falter when you wondered, "Will He really do this for me?"

Remember He is faithful even when we are not. Chose to trust Him one day at a time.

Prayer

You are faithful, Father. I choose to trust You in every area of my life. Point out those things that could hinder me from doing so. Help me to let go of them and cling to You instead. I ask this in the name of Jesus, the One who taught me how to live.

---

[15] John 14:1

TO OBEY
IS BETTER

To obey is better than sacrifice,

I Samuel 15:22b

TO OBEY IS BETTER

What comes to mind when you hear the word obey? Something you have to do whether you want to or not? Some people feel that way about God's laws. It's a bunch of rules you have to follow. The implication is often negative. But let's look at obedience from God's point of view, the positive aspect.

God wants us to obey Him because He loves us. He wants us to obey Him for our own good. He already knows what will happen if we don't. It's in our best interest to do what He says. We don't always see it that way, however.

Disobedience can be disastrous. Adam and Eve didn't obey God and it got them into a great deal of trouble. It turned their lives upside down. Sin entered the world because of their disobedience and separated them from God. Before the fall they had it all, but they lost it when they decided to disobey.

If you're a parent, you want the best for your children, no matter how old they are. You don't want them to get hurt, so you tell them to stay away from things that could harm them.

Likewise, your Heavenly Father wants His best for you. He gives you guidelines to live by. He sets the parameters. Don't look at obedience to Him as something that keeps you from doing what you want to do. Think about what God may be saving you from. What looks innocuous may not be.

God has great and wonderful plans for you, but He can only take you as far as you are willing to go with Him. You have everything to gain by obeying God and everything to lose when you don't. Ask Adam.

God also wants us to obey Him because we love Him. He doesn't force us to comply. He wants us to obey Him because we want to. It's a matter of the heart. The decision is ours to make. We have the choice of obeying or disobeying just as the first family did. We also live with the consequences of that choice like they did.

Obedience is a daily matter. We may have been obedient yesterday, but what are we going to do today? That's why having a heart for God is so important. When we do, we won't have to struggle over every decision. We know what God expects and we do it because we love Him and want to please Him. But when we push God out of our hearts, our minds are darkened and we are easily deceived. The world's ways look appealing and entice us.

What an example Jesus is to us. He obeyed His Father willingly and completely because He loved Him. When Jesus lived here on earth, He didn't run off on His own to do as He pleased. Disobedience wasn't even a consideration. Jesus lived an obedient life. He did what His Father told Him to do. "For I did not speak of my own accord, but the Father who sent me commanded me what to say and how to say it. I know that his command leads to eternal life. So whatever I say is just what the Father has told me to say."[1] His ultimate obedience led to the cross. And being found in appearance as a man, he humbled himself and became obedient to death - even death on a cross![2]

What happens when we obey God? *It shows we know Him.* We know that we have come to know him if we obey his commands. The man who says, "I know him, but does not do what he commands is a liar, and the truth is not in him." [3] We can't know God if we don't obey Him. We may know all about Him — what He's like - but we won't know Him personally or be in a close relationship with Him.

It shows we love Him. "If anyone loves me, he will obey my teaching. My Father will love him, and we will come to him and make our home with him. He who does not love me will not obey my teaching. These words you hear are not my own; they belong to the Father who sent me." [4] This is love for God: to obey his commands. And his commands are not burdensome.[5] Jesus said if we love Him, we will obey Him. When we do, He pours out His blessings on us. He lavishes us with His love. Totally undeserved, but gratefully accepted.

---

[1] John 12:49-50
[2] Philippians 2:8
[3] I John 2:3-4
[4] John 14:23
[5] I John 5:3

It also shows we believe Him. If we truly trust the Lord, we won't hesitate to do what He tells us. Obedience comes from faith. When we doubt, we tend to think it over and ponder the alternatives. We don't look at the consequences.

Obedience is essential for resting. It's not an option. Those who obey his commands live in him, and he in them.[6] They are abiding in Him and resting in Him. When we obey the Father, we are living the life He has for us, the abundant life Jesus came to give us.

Then there's the other side. And to whom did God swear that they would never enter his rest if not to those who disobeyed? [7] Disobedience separates us from God. It shuts Him out. We can't rest in Him if we don't obey Him. It's that simple. God spells it out quite plainly. He asks us: "Which way is it going to be? Yours or Mine?"

Consider what we have if we obey Him. Jesus tells us: "As the Father has loved me, so have I loved you. Now remain in my love. If you obey my commands, you will remain in my love, just as I have obeyed my Father's commands and remain in his love." [8] When we obey Him, we stay in His love and rest secure in Him.

When we comprehend and acknowledge who God is and all He has done for us, why would we deliberately decide to disobey Him? Why choose to lose all the Father has for us? Why opt for the curses instead of the blessings?

Sometimes we take obedience far too lightly. God's commands are not mere suggestions. He means what He says. Jesus tells us: "Not everyone who says to me, 'Lord, Lord,' will enter the kingdom of heaven, but only he who does the will of my Father who is in heaven. Many will say to me on that day, 'Lord, Lord, did we not prophesy in your name, and in your name drive out demons and perform many miracles?' Then I will tell them plainly, 'I never knew you. Away from me, you evildoers!'" [9] Why take a chance on missing heaven by not doing what God tells us to do?

---

[6] I John 3:24
[7] Hebrews 3:18
[8] John 15:9
[9] Matthew 7:21-23

It's interesting to note that God told Adam *not* to do one thing. Everything else was permissible. What did Adam do? The very thing God told him not to do. He chose to disobey. As a result, sin invaded the world and man has been separated from God ever since. Sin entered not only Adam's life, but ours as well. Then God told us to *do one thing* to be saved and reconciled to Him. One thing. Believe on the name of His Son, Jesus Christ, who died on a cross so we could be forgiven and restored to Him. And yet many still refuse to do the one thing God requires of them. As a result, they will miss spending eternity with Him.

Why is it so difficult for us to conform? Why can't we simply do what God says? There's still a lot of self in us. The flesh is strong. We find it hard to obey because we don't have a heart for God. When we obey, we try to do it out of duty rather than out of love for Him. Mere duty wears thin and can lead to resentment and rebellion. God promised His people Israel: 'I will give you a new heart and put a new spirit in you; I will remove from you your heart of stone and give you a heart of flesh. And I will put my Spirit in you and move you to follow my decrees and be careful to keep my laws.' [10] He wants to do the same for us today.

In the book of Ezekiel, God refers to the idols His people set up in their hearts. They openly worshiped false gods. Our idols today are hidden and far more subtle. They are anything that takes God's place in our hearts.

Jesus contrasts those who obey Him with those who don't. Hearing isn't enough. Merely thinking about it isn't sufficient. Faith requires action. We must do what He says.

"I will show you what he is like who comes to me and hears my words and puts them into practice. He is like a man building a house, who dug down deep and laid the foundation on rock. When a flood came, the torrent struck that house but could not shake it, because it was well built. But the one who hears my words and does not put them into practice is like a man who built a house on the ground without a foundation. The moment the torrent struck that house, it collapsed and its destruction was complete." [11]

---

[10] Ezekiel 36:26-27
[11] Luke 6:47-49

A favorite hymn tells us: "Trust and obey for there's no other way. There isn't any other way. Whether it's God's ultimate rest in heaven or His rest for us here on earth, we are required to trust and obey the One who calls us to that rest. He doesn't want us to miss it.

God called His chosen people obstinate, stiff-necked and stubborn. They blatantly went their own way and did their own thing. The results were disastrous. That can be a warning to us today. God offers Himself to us as He did to them. They went after the world instead. What are we going to do?

There have been times in my life when the Lord told me to do something and I obeyed; but at the moment it didn't seem that urgent. Only later did I find out how significant it really was. God's timing was perfect. Had I procrastinated, the opportunity would have passed and I would have missed it. I've asked: "Lord, why didn't you tell me how important this was? I could have missed it." His reply: "I expect you to obey me all the time in the little things as well as the big ones. You're not going to know which they are until you do them. If you are faithful to Me in the little things, then I can entrust you with the bigger ones."

When God calls me to do something, I know it's important to obey regardless of what is. When He nudges me call someone, I've learned to follow through and do it. Often I don't know what I'm going to say except, "I've had you on my heart today." The reply frequently surprises me. "Thanks so much for calling right now. I've been so discouraged today. How did you know I needed a lift.?" I didn't, but God did. If God shows me what to do and I don't do it, why should He continue to do so? If I want to get closer to Him, be led by Him and rest in Him; I need to do what He says.

When we obey God, we see Him mightily at work. How exciting that is. When our son who lives in Florida was preparing to move, we planned to go down to help him. He had an infected foot and it was difficult for him to get around. Our intention was to go the later part of the month when his lease was up. He'd checked on several apartment complexes but they weren't sure if one would be available when he needed it.

One Thursday morning during our prayer time, my husband asked out of the blue, "What about going now?" My first reaction was 'No way!' "You've got to be kidding, I answered. "I'm trying to finish writing a book before we leave at the end of the month. You and Tom (our son who lives in town) are going to the lake on Saturday to put in the pier. I thought we were going to help move Bob. Why should we go now?" We prayed about it and God confirmed Hank's feelings. His answer was, "Go Monday. Work on the book until it's finished, then wash and pack. Call Bob and tell him you'll be there Tuesday and you don't know how long you'll be staying."

We called our son to inform him of the change in plans. There was dead silence on the other end. Then he said, "I thought you were going to help me move." "We are, but we don't know when. We just found out ourselves and we don't know how long we'll be staying either." We still laugh about that. What a shock it was to all of us.

I was motivated. I finished the book, packed and we were on our way early Monday morning, the first of the month. As soon as we pulled into Bob's driveway on Tuesday, it was evident God had everything under control. We even got to see a spectacular space shot soar right over his house late that afternoon. The entire time we were there, things went like clockwork as though Someone had it all planned out. Of course, He did. We felt as though we were sitting back watching everything play out according to God's plan.

After our surprise call, Bob had phoned the apartment complex he liked best and found they would have a one bedroom apartment on the ground floor to view on the following Friday. Someone was moving out over the weekend. It was the only one available. These were hard to come by and were always snapped up quickly. He made an appointment for us to see it then. However, we decided not to wait until Friday. Wednesday morning we drove over to see the apartments. We couldn't see the vacated one since they were redecorating it, but they showed us a similar one upstairs. We gave them a deposit to hold it. We returned Friday to do the paper work and moved in Saturday afternoon. Had we not talked to the people in the office on Wednesday, the apartment would have been gone before Friday. Bob found out later the complex was completely filled. No apartments of any kind were available for two more months.

Even today, I am amazed as I look back on the events of that trip. Do you know how hard it is to find a moving truck in the middle of the busy season on such short notice? God got us a U-Haul. We picked it up at eleven Saturday morning and had it back by five that night. The weather was beautiful. God literally had everything planned out. He found us sturdy packing boxes. Furniture and a lawn mower that was no longer needed were set out at the curb and picked up immediately by those who could use them. Each day was one of expectation as we waited to see His hand at work. He is a God of details and we saw Him work them out one by one, even those we hadn't anticipated. He even provided a free pizza for moving day. We moved on Saturday, came back and cleaned up the old house and were totally unpacked and settled in the new place by the middle of the week. We left to come home on Thursday and missed the fires that ravaged the Florida coastline later that month - the time we had originally planned to be there.

Why does God go to so much trouble for us? We already know His answer. "Because I love you." That's also the reason He calls us to obey Him. Because He loves us.To obey is better by far.

To Think About:

Is it hard for you to do what God says?

What hinders you?

Do you believe He wants you to obey Him for your own good?

Do you know how much He loves you and wants His best for you?

Prayer

Father, I want to please You and obey You. Sometimes it's a struggle and I fall far short of it. Merely wanting to isn't enough. I need Your help to do it. Make me more like Jesus, the perfect example of obedience. I ask this in His name.

CHAPTER 8

THEY SHALL NEVER ENTER MY REST

*Their hearts are always going astray
and they have not known my ways.
So I declared on oath in my anger,
'They shall never enter my rest.'*

Hebrews 3:10b-11

THEY SHALL NEVER ENTER MY REST

Does God's infinite patience ever come to an end? At what point will the Creator declare, "I've had enough?"

The Lord saw how great man's wickedness on the earth had become and that every inclination of the thoughts of his heart was only evil all the time The Lord was grieved that he had made man on the earth, and his heart was filled with pain. So the Lord said, "I will wipe mankind, whom I have created from the face of the earth - men and animals, and creatures that move along the ground, and birds of the air - for I am grieved that I have made them." But Noah found favor in the eyes of the Lord.[1]

How quickly men turned from their Creator when sin entered the world. Murder invaded the first family when Cain killed his brother Abel. From there, things went downhill until they reached the lowest point of degradation when God called out, "No more." We can't begin to fathom the intense pain God felt. He was sorry He made man. He had great plans for His creation. Such high hopes for them. *But instead of turning to Him, they turned away. The things of the world were more important to them than He was.*

These people were totally given over to evil. The decadence was unbelievable. God didn't say they were somewhat bad, He said they were rotten to the core. Thoroughly evil all the time. They would never change, so He had no other choice than to wipe them out. Our omniscient God knew how things would turn out even before He made them. Yet He still created man. God was willing to subject Himself to all that pain.

Scripture says one man, Noah, found favor with the Lord. He was the one bright spot in a dark, decaying world. He alone had a heart for God. God saved him, his wife, three sons and their wives and started over again with them. The lineage carried forward. Who were those who drowned in the deluge? Noah's relatives. His family. They ridiculed him as he worked all those years on the ark God had instructed him to build. They taunted him. "What are you doing, Noah? God said what? You must be joking." They didn't believe God and they were engulfed in the flood.

---

[1] Genesis 6:5-8

He leveled Sodom and Gomorrah when they reached the pits of moral decay. Then the Lord said, "The outcry against Sodom and Gomorrah is so great and their sin so grievous that I will go down and see if what they have done is as bad as the outcry that has reached me. If not, I will know."[2] Abraham's nephew, Lot, lived in Sodom with his family. When the Lord told Abraham what He was about to do, he pleaded with God not to kill the good along with the bad. The Lord promised Abraham if ten righteous people could be found, He would not destroy it. Think about it - ten out of an entire city. What a small number in comparison to all those who lived there. But there weren't even ten righteous ones, so He destroyed it. The inhabitants of Sodom weren't going to change. There was no hope for them. God spared Lot, his wife and two daughters, however.

God was extremely angry with the Israelites in the wilderness. They felt His wrath many times. They left the land of Egypt, but Egypt never left them. In their hearts, they kept turning back. He dealt harshly with those who didn't obey Him. He made examples of them so others wouldn't follow their ways. He stopped them before the insurrection spread. Rebellion is contagious. When Korah, Dathan, Abiram and two hundred fifty well-known Israelite community leaders rose up against Moses. God put an end to them in a very dramatic way. It not only got everyone's attention, it also put the fear of God in them. They were ready to obey Him.

We need to understand, God never does anything rashly. We humans do, but He does not. He has every right to be angry, but He also has infinite patience. His plans are well thought out. God's wrath was meant to shake up His people so they would turn back to Him. His anger got their attention when nothing else could. In His mercy, God let other countries defeat the Israelites. When they had a change of heart and turned to Him once more, He heard their cries and rescued them from their captors.

So as the Holy Spirit says: "Today, if you hear His voice, do not harden your hearts as you did in the rebellion, during the time of testing in the desert, where your fathers tested and tried me and for forty years saw what I did. That is why I was angry with that generation, and I said, "Their hearts are always going astray and they have not known my

---

[2] Genesis 18:20-21

ways. So I declared on oath in my anger, 'They shall never enter my rest.' [3] They didn't enter God's rest because of their *disobedience*. It was déjà vu all over again.

Instead of the promised land, they perished in the desert. They never entered God's rest because *they didn't believe Him.* They were God's chosen people. He told them what He would do for them but the message they heard was of no value to them, because those who heard did not combine it with faith.[4]

The world had a strong pull on God's people. He called them apart to be His alone. They were His chosen people, but they didn't want to be different. They desired to be like those around them. He wanted to be their king. They sought someone else, a king like the other nations had. God said, "You yourselves have seen what I did to Egypt, and how I carried you on eagles' wings and brought you to myself. Now if you obey me fully and keep my covenant, then out of all nations you will be my treasured possession. Although the whole earth is mine, you will be for me a kingdom of priests and a holy nation." [5] What a privilege God was giving them. But they turned Him down. They rejected His offer. Instead of a kingdom of priests, He ended up with one tribe of priests, the tribe of Levi.

God wanted His people close to Him. He came down on Mount Sinai in the sight of all the people. Then Moses led the people out of the camp to meet with God, and they stood at the foot of the mountain. Mount Sinai was covered with smoke, because the Lord descended on it in fire. The smoke billowed up from it like smoke from a furnace, the whole mountain trembled violently, and the sound of the trumpet grew louder and louder. Then Moses spoke and the voice of God answered him.[6] How awesome that must have been.

These chosen ones stood in the very presence of God. When the people saw the thunder and lightning and heard the trumpet and saw the mountain in smoke, they trembled with fear. They stayed at a distance and said to Moses, "Speak to us yourself and we will listen. But do not have

---

[3] Hebrews 3:7-11
[4] Hebrews 4:3
[5] Exodus 19:4-6
[6] Exodus 19:17-19

God speak to us or we will die." [7] They had already heard God speak and they were still alive. Nothing happened to them. They weren't going to die. They simply did not want to come any closer to God. They were satisfied with an intermediary, a go-between. Let Moses talk to God, then he could tell them what God had said. They wanted it second hand, rather than hearing from God themselves.

Moses said to the people, "Do not be afraid. God has come to test you so that the fear of God will be with you to keep you from sinning." [8] But the pull of the world was stronger and led them into idolatry and other sins. *They missed God's rest, because they missed God.*

What would it take to convince God's people how much He loved them? What would He have to do to keep them from straying and missing His best for them? What would turn their hearts to Him?

At just the right time, God sent His Son into the world. God sent Jesus to come down and live among His creation. Maybe men would turn to Him now. This was the ultimate price He would pay - the life of His only Son. This was His greatest and final offer. For God so loved the world that he gave his one and only Son, that whoever believes in him shall not perish but have eternal life. For God did not send his Son into the world to condemn the world, but to save the world through him. [9]

Were people overjoyed when God did this? Were they in awe that He would do such a thing? Did they all embrace the Son and faithfully follow Him? Were the days of straying over? No.

He was in the world, and though the world was made through him, the world did not recognize him. He came to that which was his own, but his own did not receive him. [10] Instead of being hailed as the Father's Son who came to redeem them, Jesus was rejected, abused and led out to die on a cross. Yet to all who received him, to those who believed in his name, he gave the right to become children of God - children born

---

[7] Exodus 20:18-19
[8] Exodus 20:20-21
[9] John 3: 16-17
[10] John 1:10-11

not of natural descent, nor of human decision or a husband's will, but born of God.[11] God offered His ultimate rest to us through His Son Jesus Christ. An eternal one.

Several years ago, my husband and I were part of an evangelistic group sent out to tell others about Jesus Christ. We met at a church in the morning, headed out for the day, then returned late that afternoon to compare results.

One fellow told us about an experience he had. He talked with a gentleman for quite a while but to no avail. Finally he said in exasperation, " Here's my name and phone number. If you decide not to reject Jesus any longer, give me a call." The gentleman was somewhat startled. "Oh I'm not rejecting Jesus. I just haven't decided whether or not to accept Him." Many are like that indecisive man. Still on the fence. They don't realize no response is a "no" reply. They are rejecting Jesus. "Whoever believes in him is not condemned, but whoever does not believe stands condemned already because he has not believed in the name of God's one and only Son."[12] They think they have all the time in the world to decide. There's no rush. But no one knows when this world will come to an end or when his personal life on earth will be over. If you haven't done so already, *now is the moment to choose Jesus Christ.* Later may be too late.

Not only is faith vitally important, obedience is too. Jesus asked, "Why do you call me, 'Lord, Lord' and do not do what I say?" [13] *If we claim to be followers of Jesus, we need to follow Him and do what He says.*

Obedience and faith are bound together. If we don't believe God, it will be difficult for us to obey Him. We may attempt to do so out of duty, but our compliance won't last long. Sooner or later, our good intentions will fall away. We know we ought to obey, but we don't.

God offers us the greatest rest of all - an eternal one. And it is available to each of us. He doesn't want any one to miss it, so He's waiting as long as possible before He puts an end to things. The Lord is not slow

---

[11] John 1:12-13
[12] John 3:18
[13] Luke 6:46

in keeping his promise, as some understand slowness. He is patient with you, not wanting anyone to perish, but everyone to come to repentance.[14]

This world of ours is winding down. That's difficult for most to imagine. As long as we've been alive, it's always been there. When will the end come? We don't know. God doesn't tell us that. He simply says it will. Unbelief is still prevalent in the world today. So is disobedience. God didn't put up with them in the past nor will He do so now.

I believe tough times may lie ahead for us. In His mercy, God is still trying to get our attention and turn us back to Him. *He has not forgotten our sins; He wants to cleanse us from them.*

How will He do that? He's already done it through the death of His Son, Jesus, who died on a cross so we could be forgiven and cleansed. Jesus said, "I am the way and the truth and the life. No one comes to the Father except through me." [15]

We have a loving Heavenly Father who lavishes us with His love. We like that. But He is also a holy God who hates sin. We don't want to think about that aspect of Him. If He were only a God of love, we could get by with anything. He didn't need to send Jesus to die for us. If He were only a holy God, He wouldn't have bothered. He would have wiped us out. That's the whole point of Jesus' dying on the cross. To satisfy both a loving God and a holy one. Who else would do that. No one. Who else could do that? No one. We are sinners saved by His mercy and grace. We can't earn His rest. We need only to repent and accept it.

Peter tells us: But the day of the Lord will come like a thief. The heavens will disappear with a roar; the elements will be destroyed by fire, and the earth and everything in it will be laid bare.

Since everything will be destroyed in this way, what kind of people ought you to be? You ought to live holy and godly lives as you look forward to the day of God and speed its coming. That day will bring about the destruction of the heavens by fire and the elements will melt in the

---

[14] 2 Peter 3:9
[15] John 14:6

heat. But in keeping with his promise we are looking forward to a new heaven and a new earth, the home of righteousness.

So then, dear friends, since you are looking forward to this, made every effort to be found spotless, blameless and at peace with him. Bear in mind that our Lord's patience means salvation.[16] We need to get right with the Lord now. Today.

First of all, you must understand that in the last days scoffers will come, scoffing and following their own evil desires. They will say, "Where is this 'coming' he promised? Ever since our fathers died, everything goes on as it has since the beginning of creation." But they deliberately forget that long ago by God's word the heavens existed and the earth was formed out of water and by water. By these waters also the world of that time was deluged and destroyed. By the same word the present heavens and earth are reserved for fire, being kept for the day of judgment and destruction of ungodly men.[17]

There were many scoffers before the flood, but they were destroyed by the deluge. We have been warned that there will be an abundance of scoffers in the last days too. They don't expect anything to change either. Where will you be when it does? Forgiven and reconciled to the Father or taking your chances when you reject His offer of love?

A former neighbor of ours would never accept Jesus Christ. He died without changing his mind. His attitude was: "I'll take my chances. The good I've done in my life should outweigh the bad." That isn't the way it works in God's eyes. He says there is no one who does good, not even one.[18] We are all sinners who can be saved by His grace. If we don't accept His gift of salvation, there's nothing else we can do to tip the scales in our favor.

But the wicked are like the tossing sea, which cannot rest, whose waves cast up mire and mud. "There is no peace," says my God, "for the wicked." [19]

---

[16] 2 Peter 3:10-15
[17] 2 Peter 3:3-7
[18] Romans 3:12b
[19] Isaiah 57: 20-21

Contrast that with what He says about those who are Christ's. Therefore, there is now no condemnation for those who are in Christ Jesus.[20] For God was pleased to have all his fullness dwell in him, and through him to reconcile to himself all things, whether things on earth or things in heaven, by making peace through his blood, shed on the cross.[21]

When we accept Jesus Christ as Lord of our lives, His righteousness is credited to us. God looks at us through the filter of Christ's blood. There is no righteousness in us. It's all in Him. He didn't just change us. He made us brand-new. He cleansed us by His blood shed on the cross.

Those who do not accept God's indescribable gift are still dead in their sins. God offers them reconciliation through Christ's blood. If they reject it however, they cannot rest, nor will they have peace.

Imagine how God must feel. He takes no pleasure in seeing anyone miss heaven. He went to so much trouble so they don't.

---

[20] Romans 8:1
[21] Colossians 19-20

To Think About:

What have you decided to do about Jesus Christ? That's a question each of us has to answer. No one else can do it for us.

Where is He in your life?

Have you accepted Him as your Savior and Lord?

Do you believe Him?

Do you obey Him and follow Him?

Prayer

Father, thank you for sending Your Son, Jesus, to die on a cross so I might live. Because of Him, I am forgiven and cleansed. I am a new person. May my thoughts and actions reflect this. Help me to live each day for You. I pray this in the name of my Redeemer.

CHAPTER
9

A HEART FOR GOD

*The Lord does not look at
the things man looks at.
Man looks at the outward appearance,
But the Lord looks at the heart.*

I Samuel 16:7b

A HEART FOR GOD

There's a phrase I can't get out of my mind... *A heart for God.* The more I think about it, the deeper it penetrates. As I write this book, I've been saturating my thoughts with Scripture. The longer I read, the more I realize how important it is to have a heart for God. That's what I want ... a heart for Him.

What is a heart for God? How do you know when you have it? In His Word, God clearly tells us what He expects from us and what a heart for Him entails. He also gives us notable examples of those who had a heart for Him.

The first person I think of is Moses. What intimacy he had with the Lord. He talked with God. They spoke together one on one. The Lord would speak to Moses face to face, as a man speaks with his friend.[1] When Miriam and Aaron began to complain about their brother, God had this to say: "he is faithful in all my house. With him I speak face to face, clearly and not in riddles; he sees the form of the Lord. Why then were you not afraid to speak against my servant Moses?"[2] In other words, "he is my man. Who are you to talk against him?" God showed Himself to Moses, but more importantly He revealed His heart to him. He laid out His thoughts and plans before Moses.

While Moses was meeting with the Lord on the mountain for forty days and forty nights to receive His commandments, the Israelites convinced Aaron to make them a golden calf. They worshiped it instead of the one true God who led them out of Egypt. God was extremely angry with them, and rightly so. In His wrath, He told Moses He was ready to annihilate them and make a great nation out of him. "I have seen these people, the Lord said to Moses, "and they are a stiff-necked people. Now leave me alone so that my anger may burn against them and that I may destroy them. Then I will make you into a great nation." [3]

How tempting that could have been for Moses. What a test. The Israelites had caused him a great deal of grief too. He knew how God felt. Always complaining, they were never satisfied. They deserved

---

[1] Exodus 33:11a
[2] Numbers 12:7b-8
[3] Exodus 32:9-10

God's wrath. *And yet only one thing was important to Moses - God's name and reputation.* He wasn't thinking about himself. He thought about God and what He would lose if He destroyed His chosen people. (Now Moses was a very humble man, more humble than anyone else on the face of the earth.)[4] God came first in his life.

"You can't do that, God. Others would say you brought your people out of Egypt only to kill them in the desert. You weren't able do what you said you would. You couldn't get the job done. Your very name is at stake. Your reputation. You have to be true to Your word." Moses revered and honored God. He didn't want anything to besmirch His name. Nothing must sully or defile it. *Moses had God's ear because God had his heart.*

"Why should the Egyptians say, 'It was with evil intent that he brought them out, to kill them in the mountains and to wipe them off the face of the earth?' Turn from your fierce anger; relent and do not bring disaster on your people." [5]

Moses reminded God of His covenant with Abraham, Isaac and Jacob in which He swore their descendants would be as numerous as the stars in the sky and He would give them the land He promised. Then Moses went a step further. "But now, please forgive their sin - but if not, then blot me out of the book you have written." [6] How many people do you know who could say that and mean it?

Since then, no prophet has risen in Israel like Moses, whom the Lord knew face to face, who did all those miraculous signs and wonders the Lord sent him to do in Egypt — to Pharaoh and to all his officials and to his whole land.[7] Moses had a heart for God.

When I consider those who had a heart for God, I also think about Abraham. He was called God's friend. What a privilege to be called a friend of God. His name is listed in the Hall of Faith in the eleventh chapter of Hebrews. Abraham waited twenty-five years for God's promise to be fulfilled concerning a son to be born to Sarah and him. He believed God and this was credited to him as righteousness.

---

[4] Numbers 12:3
[5] Exodus32:12
[6] Exodus 32:32
[7] Deuteronomy 34:10-11

Later God told him to sacrifice that same son on the altar. As a parent, I can imagine the anguish Abraham must have felt. "I love you Lord, but don't ask me to do that. I've waited so long for this son and now you want to take him away." But he didn't say that. He didn't hesitate when God commanded him to kill Isaac, the son of the promise. The son through whom the nations would be blessed. He obeyed God. Abraham had a heart for God.

What about David? When Samuel was looking for God's replacement of King Saul, God told him: "The Lord does not look at the things man looks at. Man looks at the outward appearance, but the Lord looks at the heart." [8] Samuel told Saul: "the Lord has sought out a man after his own heart and appointed him leader of his people, because you have not kept the Lord's command." [9] That young man was David. David had a heart for God.

Through the prophet, Nathan, God said to David: 'I took you from the pasture and from following the flock to be ruler over my people Israel. I have been with you wherever you have gone, and I have cut off all your enemies from before you. Now I will make your name great, like the names of the greatest men of the earth...Your house and your kingdom will endure forever before me; your throne will be established forever.' [10]

David prayed: "And now, Lord God, keep forever the promise you have made concerning your servant and his house. Do as you promised, so that your name will be great forever. Then men will say, 'The Lord Almighty is God over Israel!' And the house of your servant David will be established before you." [11]

God's Son was of the lineage of David. The angel Gabriel told Mary she would give birth to a son and name him Jesus. "He will be great and will be called the Son of the Most High. The Lord God will give him the throne of his father David, and he will reign over the house of Jacob forever; his kingdom will never end."[12]

---

[8] I Samuel 16:7b
[9] I Samuel 13: 14b
[10] 2 Samuel 7:8-9, 16
[11] 2 Samuel 7:25-26
[12] Luke 1:32-33

Consider Paul. The one who ruthlessly tracked down the followers of Jesus Christ, became one of His greatest advocates. He proclaimed: But whatever was to my profit I now consider loss for the sake of Christ. What is more, I consider everything a loss compared to the surpassing greatness of knowing Christ Jesus my Lord, for whose sake I have lost all things. I consider them rubbish, that I may gain Christ and be found in him, not having a righteousness of my own that comes from the law, but that which is through faith in Christ - the righteousness that comes from God and is by faith.[13]

Paul also declared: "I have been crucified with Christ and I no longer live, but Christ lives in me. The life I live in the body, I live by faith in the Son of God, who loved me and gave himself for me." [14] *The persistent persecutor became the passionate proponent.* Paul had a heart for God.

These are but a few who had a heart for God. What were they like? Were they perfect? No. They all made mistakes just as we do. Some of their sins were very costly. But these men were sinners who repented before God and He forgave them. This gives us hope today. As God forgave them, so He forgives us. They loved Him with all their heart. Scripture tells us: For as he thinketh in his heart, so is he: [15] *That's where it all begins... in the heart.*

If we're going to rest in the Lord, we need to have a heart for Him. What does the Lord ask us to do? What does He expect from us? A teacher of the law asked Jesus what the most important commandment was. Jesus answered him. "Love the Lord your God with all your heart and with all your soul and with all your mind and with all your strength." [16] Halfway doesn't do it. God wants us to love Him completely. Entirely. Totally. He doesn't want a mere piece of us. He wants all of us. He tells us we can't love the world and Him. We can't have it both ways. It doesn't work. The Israelites tried that and soon they were engulfed in worshiping other gods. *God wants an undivided heart.* One that is all His.

---

[13] Philippians 3:7-9
[14] Galatians 2:20
[15] Proverbs 23:7 KJ
[16] Mark 12:30

As Moses instructed the people of Israel, he said: And now, O Israel, what does the Lord your God ask of you but to fear the Lord your God, to walk in all his ways, to love him , to serve the Lord your God with all your heart and with all your soul and to observe the Lord's commands and decrees that I am giving you today for your own good?[17]

God told that to His people again and again. He kept repeating it so they wouldn't miss it. His commands were to be written on their hearts. They responded "We will do whatever you say." But their compliance turned out to be little more than lip service.

God spoke of all the promises and blessings He had for His chosen ones if only they would obey Him. He also told them quite plainly what would happen if they did not. Why would anyone choose not to obey God? The contrast between the blessings and the curses was staggering. It was a matter of life or death.

"See, I set before you today life and prosperity, death and destruction. For I command you today to love the Lord your God, to walk in his ways, and to keep his commands, decrees and laws; then you will live and increase, and the Lord your God will bless you in the land you are entering to possess." [18] Then He said: "Now choose life so that you and your children may live and that you may love the Lord your God, listen to his voice, and hold fast to him. For the Lord is your life." [19]

This is the crux of the matter: God's chosen people tried to obey Him out of a sense of duty rather than out of love for Him. They didn't have a heart for God and they missed His rest. Duty often breeds resentment and rebellion and it wasn't long before they strayed from God. Duty sees obedience as a burden, while love considers it a privilege to please the one you serve. There's a vast difference between the two both in perspective and results.

You and I can also be ensnared in this trap today. Mere duty doesn't work. If we simply follow the rules without a heart for God, we will stumble under their burden. We follow His ways because we love Him. As we do, He reveals Himself to us more and more and draws us ever closer to Him.

---

[17] Deuteronomy 10:12
[18] Deuteronomy 30:15-16
[19] Deuteronomy 30:19-20a

Will we have to give up anything in order to have a heart for God? Yes. He asks us to give up those things that hinder our relationship with Him. It may be different for each of us. It could be attitudes, habits, priorities, the use of our time, activities we take part in or even how we spend our money. For the rich young ruler, his wealth got in the way. God doesn't change us all at once, but He gently molds and remakes us into what He wants us to be.

Sometimes it's the little things that get in the way of our relationship with Him. It could be a matter of how we use our time. I enjoy knitting. When I was nine, I persuaded my grandmother to teach me how to knit. I've been knitting ever since. It's relaxing and productive at the same time. Whenever there was a spare moment, I'd pick up my needles, do a few more rows and soon another sweater would be completed. One day, the Lord asked me if I would be willing to give up knitting for Him. There was nothing wrong with it, *He just wanted me to spend more time with Him so I could get to know Him better.* I put it aside. I didn't get rid of anything, I just stashed it away in a drawer in case this was a temporary thing. It wasn't. Sometime later, He announced it was time to give away all the skeins of yarn I had purchased, my many knitting books, and a wide assortment of needles. Out they went.

Several years later, the Lord approached me about giving up TV. "Would you do this for Me? "I didn't watch much TV, but I had a few favorite programs I enjoyed. I looked forward to seeing them each week. At first when I gave them up, it was a little hard seeing my husband watch those same shows when I couldn't. Then I realized if my giving up TV was that important to the Lord, it was that important to me too. *It wasn't so much what He had me give up, but more a matter of what He gave me instead. More of Him.*

I've found it is vitally important to nurture my relationship with the Lord. This is prime time and the most important part of my day. It keeps me focused on Him and prepares me for what lies ahead. It also helps me retain the proper perspective and priorities in my life. Not only do I relish my time with the Lord, I consistently, persistently guard it. Without a daily time with Him, it's easy to be distracted. Let one thing interfere with it, and there will be others.

Can we lose our heart for God? Solomon is an example of one whose attention was deflected and diverted elsewhere. When Solomon became king after his father David died, he asked God for wisdom to be a good ruler and judge over the people. God was pleased with his request and made him the wisest man on earth. He also made him the wealthiest. Solomon was greatly esteemed. People came from far and wide to see him. *Solomon had it all.* But he became sidetracked and turned away from God. As Solomon grew old, his wives turned his heart after other gods, and his heart was not fully devoted to the Lord his God, as the heart of David his father had been.[20] His many foreign wives led him into idolatry. He did evil in the Lord's sight. He no longer had an undivided heart for God.

Solomon, the wisest and wealthiest man in the world, wrote: "Meaningless! Meaningless! Everything is meaningless!"[21] It's interesting to see how he concluded the book of Ecclesiastes. Now all has been heard; here is the conclusion of the matter: Fear God and keep his commandments, for this is the whole duty of man. For God will bring every deed into judgment, including every hidden thing, whether it is good or evil.[22] He also wrote in Proverbs: Above all else, guard your heart, for it is the wellspring of life.[23] *Solomon failed to follow his own advice.*

How will you and I know if we have a heart for God? Here are some questions we may need ask ourselves: Do I care more about His name than my own? Is what He wants more important than what I want? Does He have first place in my life? Do I obey Him because I love Him or just out of duty? Am I single minded or is my loyalty divided between Him and the world? Do I love Him with all my heart?

When you have a heart for God, you know you are the richest person in the world. In Him, you have it all!

---

[20] I Kings 11:4
[21] Ecclesiastes 12:8
[22] Ecclesiastes 12:13-14
[23] Proverbs 4:23

To Think About:

Do you have a heart for God?

Is He first in your life?

Are you totally committed to Him?

Are you willing to give up those things He asks you to - things that might hinder your relationship with Him?

Prayer

Father, give me an undivided heart. I want to please You, not the world. Change me in any way You desire. Help me to live my life for You. I pray this expectantly in Jesus' name.

CHAPTER 10

COUNT YOUR BLESSINGS

Be at rest once more, O my soul,
For the Lord has been good to you.

Psalm 116:7

COUNT YOUR BLESSINGS

Do you ever get discouraged? I do when my eyes are focused on the circumstances rather than on the Creator. When I allow the zingers that come my way to temporarily undermine and weaken my faith in Him. Doubt sneaks in and clouds my viewpoint. I no longer see the bigger picture, but instead I'm enmeshed in the immediate problems. I have tunnel vision. I'm short sighted and forget that my Father never leaves me or forsakes me. I can be beaten down by despair or choose to rise above the challenges, knowing that no matter what lies ahead, He can handle it. I opt for the latter, set my sights on Him and I am at rest once more.

In the book, IN HIS HANDS, I related how a routine x-ray revealed a large tumor in my chest that required surgery. Upon learning of my family's history of cancer, the physician wanted to remove the tumor immediately. "As I sat there on the examining table reflecting on what the surgeon had said, I heard the voice of the Lord so clearly. *'It's all right. I am with you.'* I'd never felt such love before. And peace. I was very aware of his presence. He was so reassuring."[1] That was a time when I simply rested in Him. I didn't know what the future might bring, but I knew He would be there.

One thing that helped tremendously was looking back and recalling the times when I knew the Lord had touched my life. As they came to mind, I wrote each one down so I could draw strength and hope from them. What a boost they were. They gave me a lift when I needed it. How encouraging it was to see that the Lord had been there for me all along. Here was concrete evidence that He truly cared. *Counting my blessings built up my faith.*

It's so easy to look at what isn't, rather than what is. To focus on what we lack instead of what we have. The Apostle Paul said: I have learned to be content whatever the circumstances. I know what it is to be in need, and I know what it is to have plenty. I have learned the secret of being content in any and every situation, whether well fed or hungry, whether living in plenty or in want.[2] That isn't something that comes

---

[1] IN HIS HANDS p 17
[2] Philippians 4:11-12

easily. Paul learned it. He learned to rest in the Lord regardless of the situation. If only we would do the same. What a tremendous difference that could make in our lives. He wrote those words when he was in prison.

Scripture tells us: Be joyful always; pray continually; give thanks in all circumstances for this is God's will for you in Christ Jesus.[3] That's one of the verses the Lord has deeply impressed upon me. Do I always do it? No. Does He remind me of it when I don't? Often. Does it make a difference in my life when I do? Yes. It means I have my eyes on Him instead of on me.

The other day, I had the opportunity to talk with a woman I've known for years. Her family has been through many trying times and continues to do so. As she brought me up to date on what was happening, she concluded, "God is good." She could have been bitter, she could have thrown up her hands in despair, but instead her eyes were on the Lord, her hope and help in these times of need. What an inspiration she is to others. What a witness for Christ. That's what God had in mind when He said to be thankful in all circumstances regardless of what they are. Give thanks to the Lord, for he is good; his love endures forever. [4]

Each morning when my husband and I come together to be with the Lord, we begin with praise and thanksgiving as we recall those things for which we are grateful. Most of all, we are grateful for Him, the One who lavishes us with His love. Sometimes we start out rather slowly, but before long we pick up speed as we remember more and more of what He has done in our lives and in the lives of our family and friends. Big things as well as little ones that have meant so much to us. It's exciting to realize these would not have happened, had it not been for the Lord. I think of the details involved and all the trouble He went to in order to bring them about. He has a lot invested in us.

Thanking God is far more important than we realize. This speaks volumes about our relationship with Him. It's easy to thank Him when He answers our prayers the way we want Him to. We don't need to be prompted to thank Him when everything is going well, although sometimes we don't even do that. But we can't seem to find the words to do

---

[3] I Thessalonians 5:16-18
[4] I Chronicles 16:34

so in the middle of our adversities. Surely, God doesn't expect us to thank Him then, does He? Yes. He said in *all* circumstances. That means in the good times as well as the bad. It doesn't matter whether or not we feel like doing it. In many cases, it's a real sacrifice, but He says our sacrifice of thanks honors Him. By him therefore let us offer the sacrifice of praise to God continually, that is, the fruit of our lips giving thanks to his name.[5]

Giving thanks changes us. It negates the negative and gives us hope instead, regardless of the circumstances. They may not change, but we do. We respond differently to them. Our attitude undergoes a transformation. *Fear gives way to faith. Uncertainty finds security in Him.* And before long, what may have started out as little more than lip service is replaced by pure gratitude that comes from the very depths of our hearts.

Giving thanks is good for our health. I feel better when I take time to thank the Lord. There's an inner peace and I'm filled with joy. My outlook is much brighter. It's positive and full of hope. A cheerful heart is good medicine, but a crushed spirit dries up the bones.[6]

As we look at Scripture, we notice it says to thank the Lord as we pray. *Before He does a thing!* Do not be anxious about anything, but in everything, by prayer and petition, with thanksgiving, present your requests to God.[7]

That puts a whole new slant on it. It takes a lot of faith to thank Him when we don't know what will happen. Jesus did that. He thanked His Father before He did a thing. So should we. This implies we trust Him to work out His very best in the situation facing us. *Giving thanks takes hold of it now.*

Giving thanks pleases our Father. It also draws us closer to Him. A grateful heart doesn't take God for granted but it appreciates all He does. A grateful heart is also an expectant one and sees Him in action. He owes us nothing, yet in His mercy He gives us His all.

---

5 Hebrews 13:15 KJ
6 Proverbs 17:22
7 Philippians 4:6

Giving thanks to the Lord is a witness to others. Sometimes our greatest witness comes as we simply trust Him and stand firm in Him during the tough times. We thank Him for being our refuge and strength and seeing us through them. People look to see if what we say is backed up by how we live. Does our walk match our talk? When it does, our faith endures and we don't give up because our hope is in Him.

I often reflect on this verse in Habakkuk: Though the fig tree does not bud and there are no grapes on the vines, though the olive crop fails and the fields produce no food, though there are no sheep in the pen and no cattle in the stalls, yet I will rejoice in the Lord. I will be joyful in God my Savior.[8] Though everything is going wrong, I will be joyful and thankful in the middle of the adversities. That's hard to do, but I've seen Him turn things around when I was. The more you do it, the easier it becomes.

In I Corinthians, Paul points to the Israelites when they were in the desert as an example of what *not* to do. Instead of thanking God for what He had already done, they continually grumbled. Although they had seen God's mighty hand at work through the plagues, the exodus from Egypt and the parting of the Red Sea plus numerous other miracles, they chose a life of complaining. They were never satisfied. They hated the manna. It wasn't good enough. They wanted meat instead. Carping became a habit, a way of life for them. Their hearts became hardened and they rebelled against God and Moses whom He had chosen to lead them. God called them a stiff-necked people and He was very angry with them. We don't like to be around negative people. Neither does God.

Grumbling is an easy trap to fall into and it's contagious. I've been in groups where one person can quickly sway the tenor of the meeting from positive to negative with a few choice words. The mood suddenly changes and people wonder why.

Thanksgiving increases our faith and protects us from the evil one. On the other hand, grumbling tears down our faith and leads us away from God. It plays right into Satan's hands and gives him an inroad into our lives. We need to keep our minds and hearts on the Lord instead of listening to the devil's drivel. It's a choice we make every day. The more we praise and thank our Father, the more we will see. It's a matter of attitude. God looks at the heart.

---

[8] Habakkuk 3:17-18

A scripture in Romans comes to mind: For although they knew God, they neither glorified him as God nor gave thanks to him, but their thinking became futile and their foolish hearts were darkened. [9] They exchanged the truth of God for a lie, and worshiped and served created things rather than the Creator - who is forever praised.[10] He let them go their own way and do their own thing. And they missed out on what God had for them.

Is thanking God really that important? Yes. It's all wrapped up in our relationship with Him. If we truly have *a heart for God,* we will be filled with gratitude for Him. We are to: Enter his gates with thanksgiving and his courts with praise; give thanks to him and praise His name. [11] We will be more aware of who He is and what He does for us. If we don't have a heart for Him, we will look at the gifts rather than the Giver. I've been around people who believe God owes them something. They deserve it. Like the Israelites in the desert, they are never satisfied. They always want more. God owes us nothing, but in His great mercy He freely gives to us. He doesn't need our thanks. It won't make or break Him. He can get along without it, *but we can't.*

It pleases our Father when we appreciate Him. But more than that, an attitude of gratitude means our hearts are right with Him. It puts things in the proper perspective. We begin to realize all we have is a gift from Him. David was right when he said to God: "Everything comes from you." [12] He is the source of our blessings. Give Him the credit. Give Him thanks.

What do we have to thank our Father for? But thanks be to God! He gives us the victory through our Lord Jesus Christ.[13] Thanks be to God for his indescribable gift.[14] *Jesus Christ is His greatest gift of all.*

---

[9] Romans 1:21
[10] Romans 1:25
[11] Psalm 100:4
[12] 1 Chronicles 29:14
[13] 1 Corinthians 15:57
[14] 2 Corinthians 9:15

To Think About:

Do you take time to count your blessings?

How does this encourage you?

Are you content with what you have or do you look at what you lack?

Prayer

I have so much to be thankful for, Father. Open my eyes to see all that I have in You. Help me to be content with what I have rather looking at what I lack. Enable me to make everyday Thanksgiving Day. I love you. I pray in the name of Jesus, Your greatest gift of all.

CHAPTER
11

NO SWEAT

*For anyone who enters God's rest
also rests from his own work,
just as God did from his.*

Hebrews 4:10

NO SWEAT

Resting is hard for some of us. A former neighbor found it extremely difficult to rest. If you were doing any kind of repair work around the house, he came over to help you without your even asking him to. He felt guilty if he didn't. All his neighbors loved him. At night he would come dragging home from work, completely beat, but that didn't deter him. If a project awaited his attention, he had to tackle it right then. No matter how hard his wife tried, she was unable to persuade him to do otherwise. He needed rest, but he couldn't bring himself to do that. It was impossible for him to sit still. Relaxing wasn't part of his makeup. When a physician told him he needed knee surgery , he kept putting it off because he dreaded being incapacitated. The thought of not being able to get around and do things was more than he could handle. He was a do-er and his self esteem was tied to what he accomplished.

Some of us are like that in our relationship to God. It's all about what we can do for Him. But that isn't what He wants from us. He wants us. He calls us to surrender to Him and rest in Him. He wants to do His work through us as we do. Otherwise, we get in His way and hinder Him.

Mary and Martha were dear friends of Jesus. When He came to their home in Bethany for a visit, Martha was bustling about getting everything ready, while Mary sat at His feet, drinking in every word He said. But Martha was distracted by all the preparations that had to be made. She came to him and asked, "Lord, don't you care that my sister has left me to do the work by myself? Tell her to help me!" [1]

I can understand the frustration Martha felt. There was a house to clean and food to prepare for their guest. After all , they were hosting the Lord. She wanted to do it right and she needed help to do so. Her sister seemed totally oblivious and unconcerned about it. I think about our holiday celebrations today and the many preparations that need to be completed. If we don't do them, who will? Guests expect a clean house and plenty to eat, don't they? Besides, hungry husbands are not happy ones. They like to be fed. But sometimes like Martha, we take on more than we need to and it becomes a drudgery rather than a joy. We're too busy with all the details and too tired to enjoy the occasion.

---

[1] Luke 10:40

How did Jesus reply to Martha's request? Did He side with Martha and say, "You're right. You are doing all the work. Mary should be helping you. I'll tell her so. I'm hungry and I look forward to one of your scrumptious meals." Jesus didn't say that.

I think Martha was surprised by His answer. She expected Him to agree with her. "Martha, Martha," the Lord answered, "you are worried and upset about many things, but only one thing is needed. Mary has chosen what is better, and it will not be taken away from her." [2]

Instead of putting Mary down and reprimanding her, Jesus said she had things in the proper perspective, the right order. She knew what the most important thing was and she did it. He wasn't telling Martha not to fix a meal. That was expected. People needed to be fed. A good hostess provided food for her guests. Jesus said she was upset and worried about a lot of things. The harder she worked, the more upset she became when she saw Mary enjoying her time with the Lord instead of helping her. Like Martha, we too can get so caught up in all our activities, we end up ignoring our guests. We forget our primary goal is to spend time with them and make them feel welcome. If we're harried hosts who constantly hustle about doing things, they won't feel comfortable.

What might have happened if Martha had taken time out to enjoy Jesus too? Her mood would have changed as she basked in the Lord's presence. He had much to teach His friends and followers. Time was short. Soon He would be going back to His Father. He wanted to make certain they understood what His coming was all about. Only one thing was needed now - being with Him, listening to Him, learning from Him. There would be plenty of time for other things when He was gone. After being in Jesus' presence, Martha would have been refreshed. The work she had to do would still get done. But instead of a heavy burden that weighed her down, it would be a joyful privilege to serve the Lord.

At times I'm Martha and other times I'm Mary. There's some of both in most of us. But through the years, the Lord has been teaching me how important it is to just be with Him and to rest in Him. That must come first. All the things I have to do are nothing compared with that. *They can wait, but He can't.*

---

[2] Luke 10:41-42

Sometimes we forget the Lord as we carry out His work. Our top priority gets shunted to the background. Martha was a good worker, a solid citizen. You could count on her to get things done. We admire her zeal and industriousness. But Jesus said only one thing was needed - being with Him. He says the same thing to us today. *When we're in His presence, He wants our attention, not our activities.* Self effort doesn't count with Him. Through the years, I've learned that my self effort amounts to nothing. It's all wood, hay and stubble. Only what we do in His power and strength lasts.

We can also learn something from the temple priests who ministered to the Lord. When they enter the gates of the inner court, they are to wear linen clothes; they must not wear any woolen garment while ministering at the gates of the inner court or inside the temple. They are to wear linen turbans on their heads and linen undergarments around their waists. They must not wear anything that makes them perspire.[3] They were clothed in linen rather than wool. Linen doesn't cause sweating. Wool does. God doesn't want any perspiring in His presence. He doesn't want our self effort. What we do in the flesh hinders Him. He wants us to rest in Him so He can do His work through us. It makes a great difference when we do. What a relief it is and how free we are when we learn this.

But God chose the foolish things of the world to shame the wise; God chose the weak things of the world to shame the strong. He chose the lowly things of this world and the despised things - and the things that are not - to nullify the things that are, so that no one may boast before him.[4] That no flesh should glory in his presence.[5] Therefore, as it is written: "Let him who boasts boast in the Lord."[6] We're to brag about Him, not ourselves.

Have you noticed those moving walkways at airports? They're a tremendous help when you're hurrying from one end of the terminal to catch a flight at the other. Especially if you're weighed down with a lot of baggage. As soon as I step on one, I put down my heavy tote, relax and stand there until I reach my destination. The walkway moves me right along. But there's always someone who rushes past me loaded

---

[3] Ezekiel 44:17-18
[4] I Corinthians 1:27-29
[5] I Corinthians 1:29 KJ
[6] I Corinthians 1:31

with luggage. He struggles to keep from dropping it as he charges ahead. I wonder why he even bothers with the moving walkway when he insists upon walking the walkway and toting his tote himself. He certainly doesn't derive much benefit from it.

Some of us are that way with God. There's still a lot of self-effort in us. He says to rest from our own work if we're going to rest in Him. He tries to make it easier for us, but we insist upon struggling on our own. It's hard for us to admit we need help, but that's the first step we must take if we are to have the rest He promises us. The Lord knows when we're tired and bogged down and He calls to us, "Come to me. Take my yoke. Hook up with me. Learn from me. See how I do it. My yoke is easy and my load is light." There's a very simple test we can take to know if we're joined with Him or we're still trying to do things on our own. If the burden is heavy and we're straining under it's weight, we're probably doing it in our own strength rather than in His.

The world considers it a sign of weakness if we have to lean on someone else. It's a case of do it yourself. Try hard enough and you can do anything. What does God say about it? Trust in the Lord with all your heart and lean not on your own understanding; in all your ways acknowledge him, and he will make your paths straight.[7] He also tells us: He who trusts in himself is a fool.[8] Admitting our weakness is a sign of maturity as we realize our limitations and turn to Him, the One who is strong.

---

[7] Proverbs 3:5-6
[8] Proverbs 28:26a

To Think About:

Is it hard for God to get your attention? Do you have many distractions in your life?

Are you a Mary or a Martha? Which would you like to be?

Why do you think Jesus answered Martha the way He did?

What do you think He would say to you today?

Prayer

Father, forgive me for putting other things ahead of you and letting them crowd you out of my life. Help me to put you first every day. Nothing is more important than that. Jesus told Martha only one thing is needed. That's what I want - to be with You. It's in the name of Jesus, the Good Teacher, I pray.

CHAPTER 12

BUT PATIENCE ISN'T ONE OF MY VIRTUES!

Rest in the Lord,
And wait patiently for him:

Psalm 37:7 KJ

BUT PATIENCE ISN'T ONE OF MY VIRTUES!

"Are we there yet?" How many times have parents heard that one? The trip hasn't even started yet, the car is still in the driveway and your children want to know how long it's going to take. Children are notorious for their lack of patience, but they're not the only ones. We adults are too. Age has nothing to do with it. Older people don't like to wait either. Waiting isn't easy. In this world of instant gratification, we want what we want now, not later.

For most of us, patience is not one of our virtues. On a scale of 1 to 10, we're near the bottom. We readily admit we don't like to wait. It doesn't take much for us to lose our cool. A long, slowly moving checkout line at the grocery store can undo us. We size up the situation, decide which one is the fastest and begin unloading our cart. When the person in front of us begins pulling out an endless stack of coupons to redeem, we realize our dreadful error. We made a bad call and we're stuck with it. Others are in line behind us.

How about road construction? There's a great deal of that around our city now. Traffic is down to a crawl or stopped completely. Often it's backed up for miles. Nothing is moving. When it finally does, things inch forward at a snail's pace. It's interesting to watch drivers' reactions. Some lay on the horn to release their frustration. Others frantically search for a shortcut or way around it while a few are resigned to their fate knowing they're going to be late for work again.

We came face to face with road rage the other day. The highway near our home is an extremely busy especially one with all the trucks who consider it a race track. We were stopped waiting for the oncoming traffic to clear out so we could turn left onto a side road leading to our home. In doing so, you not only pray the driver behind you is aware you have stopped but that he also passes you on the right hand lane provided for this instead of plowing into you. Recently, a fatal accident occurred a few miles down the road when a semi wasn't paying attention and did just that. As we waited to turn, a flatbed truck whizzed past us and the driver yelled out a long string of expletives at us. We had inconvenienced him. He was miffed because he had to slow down a little.

Sometimes eating out can be a hassle. Not only do you have to wait a long time for a table, but once you're seated, the service is notoriously poor. You're certain they have completely forgotten you. Hope springs forth, however, when the waiter comes to take your order, but soon fades. Placing it is one thing. Getting it is quite another. After what seems like an eternity, you are finally served. You vow you will never go to that restaurant again. Fabulous food does not make up for the frustration you feel.

We recently sold our lake cottage in the northern part of the state. Through the years, we learned that things were geared at a much slower pace there than at home. It took us a while to get used to it. We learned to be more patient. People were not in a hurry. Nothing was so pressing that it had to be done immediately. It was more relaxed and laid back. Each time we headed to the lake, we used the hundred mile trip to unwind so we would be in sync with them.

The Bible gives us some good examples of patience. Abraham waited twenty-five years for God to fulfill His promise that he and Sarah would have a son and all the world would be blessed through him. What does the Scripture say? "Abraham believed God and it was credited to him as righteousness." [1] There were times during those years when Abraham and Sarah took things into their own hands, some with disastrous results, but Abraham is listed in God's Hall of Faith. Can you imagine waiting twenty-five years to see a promise fulfilled? He is to be commended not only for his faith but also for his patience.

What about Moses? Raised as the child of Pharaoh's sister, Moses was trained in all the ways of the Egyptians. Well educated and self confident, he knew he would lead his people out of bondage. But when he tried to help matters along by killing an Egyptian who was beating a Hebrew, Moses was forced to flee to Midian to escape Pharaoh's wrath. He married, had a family and stayed there forty years tending his father-in-law's flocks. During that time, God was at work in Moses preparing him to lead the Israelites out of Egypt. Forty years is a long time.

Later in the desert, the Lord said to Moses, "Come up to me on the mountain and stay here, and I will give you the tablets of stone, with the law and commands I have written for their instruction." [2] When Moses

---

[1] Romans 4:3
[2] Exodus 24:12

went up on the mountain, the cloud covered it, and the glory of the Lord settled on Mount Sinai. For six days the cloud covered the mountain, and on the seventh day the Lord called to Moses from within the cloud. To the Israelites, the glory of the Lord looked like a consuming fire on top of the mountain. Then Moses entered the cloud as he went on up the mountain. And he stayed on the mountain forty days and forty nights.[3] What do you suppose Moses was thinking about as He waited to be summoned into God's presence?

God called Moses to come to Him, but He made him wait six days. On the seventh day Moses entered the cloud and went to Him. Then he stayed on the mountain forty days and nights with the Lord. When I consider the relationship, the intimacy, Moses had with the Lord, the privilege afforded him, I am in awe. The Bible tells us there was no one else like Moses.

Why did God make Moses wait? During those days of waiting, other things began to fade away and his focus was entirely on God. His heart was being prepared to come into God's very presence, to be taught by the Lord Almighty Himself.

Why do we need to wait patiently for the Lord? What happens as we do? A time of waiting is necessary. We can't be engrossed in the things of the world one minute and expect to jump into the things of God the next. There needs to be a transition. In the process of waiting, our attitudes begin to change. Instead of thinking about ourselves and what relates to us, we turn our thoughts to God — who He is and what He is about. We shift from the mundane to the sublime, from mere man to the Almighty One. We let go of the distractions that get in the way. God is getting us ready for what is to come. He is changing us and preparing us for what lies ahead. He quiets our soul. "Be still, and know that I am God."[4] "Listen. Drink in what I am teaching you. Learn it well"

Have you ever wondered why answers to some prayers take so long? Why doesn't the Lord answer them immediately? After all, He is God and there is nothing too difficult for Him. He does answer some quickly, almost as soon as the words have left our lips. Others take longer as he works not only in the heart of the one prayed for but also in the heart of the prayer as well.

---

[3] Exodus 24:15-18
[4] Psalm 46:10

My brother, Tom, who lived in California was diagnosed with cancer. We were the last ones left in our family. He tried various treatments, but nothing seemed to work. I was concerned about his relationship with the Lord... his salvation, and I took that concern to the Lord. "You can't let him die apart from you, Lord. Send someone to lead him to you." I knew the Lord was going to send me. I began praying fervently for Tom. One month turned into another and another. I kept asking the Lord when I was to go. Whenever I posed that question, His answer was always "Be ready, but wait." I've heard that a lot in my life, but I've also learned God's timing is perfect. So I continued to pray and wait. Eight months later, He said it was time. I called my sister-in-law and told her I was coming. She was about to call me as Tom was getting progressively worse.

When I arrived, I found my brother consumed with fear. All his life he'd been afraid of dying from cancer. His fears were being confirmed. He was very glad I came. I gently began telling him about Jesus and how much He meant to me. I told him how much Jesus loved him and was there for him. Before he left to go for radiation late that afternoon , I prayed with Tom, and asked Jesus to hold his hand as he got his treatment. He dreaded those sessions. They made him extremely ill and wiped him out. When I finished praying he said, I've never heard anyone pray like you do. You act like God hears your prayers and Jesus is right here with us." "That's right," I replied. The next morning when I came back to the hospital to see him, he told me: "You know that worked. It wasn't so bad this time."

The days passed much too quickly and it was time for me to return home. On my way to the airport, I stopped by the hospital to see Tom one last time. He accepted Jesus Christ as Lord of his life. Eight days later, he died. During those months of praying for my brother, God built up my faith so I could believe Him for what He wanted to do. He was also preparing Tom's heart so he was ready to accept Jesus as his Savior and Lord. God's timing was perfect. Had I gone earlier, my brother wouldn't have been ready. Later would have been too late. His family said he changed during those last few days. He found a peace he'd been looking for all his life.

Have you ever wondered about the many details God works out in answer to prayer? Time after time, I am amazed at how perfectly He fits pieces together to give us His best. What seems simple to us requires intricate planning on His part to bring it about.

Whenever we talk about patience, we must look at our Heavenly Father, the epitome of patience. What a contrast there is between *God's infinite patience and man's impatience.* How often God's chosen people turned from Him to others, yet when they cried out to Him, He gathered them to Himself again and again. Today, we often grieve Him too. Yet His patience endures and He forgives us again and again. Is there any patience greater than God's? No and there never will be. He has all the time in the world. And He knows the outcome - how it's all going to turn out. Scripture tells us: The Lord is not slow in keeping his promise, as some understand slowness. He is patient with you, not wanting anyone to perish, but everyone to come to repentance.[5] Bear in mind that our Lord's patience means salvation,...[6]

I was talking to our son, Bill, the other day. He's job hunting and has completely committed this to the Lord. So far his resumes and interviews have not brought the desired results, but he knows the Lord has His job for him in His perfect timing. As we discussed this, he said, "If only I knew *when,* it would make it so much easier." Not knowing when is hard. I can understand that. It's the uncertainty, the not knowing that gets to us.

As I write this book, my husband and I have been in a holding pattern for months, waiting for the Lord to act in our lives. It's not a question of *if,* but *when.* We know He wants His best for us and He alone knows what that is. For us, the temptation is to try to help Him. But He doesn't need our help. He knows exactly what to do and when to do it. He won't wait one second longer than necessary to bring about what He desires. In the meantime,we rest in Him and wait patiently.

---

[5] 2 Peter 3:9
[6] 2 Peter 3:15a

To Think About:

Is waiting hard for you?

What things are especially difficult to wait for?

What do you do while you're waiting?

Are you anxious or expectant?

What are the benefits of waiting patiently?

Prayer

You have infinite patience, Father, but I'm not a very patient person. Thank You for changing me. Don't let me run ahead of You. Help me to wait for Your perfect timing. I pray this in the name of Jesus who did everything according to Your time.

CHAPTER 13

RESTING MEANS RELEASING

Commit to the Lord whatever you do,
and your plans will succeed.

Proverbs 16:3

RESTING MEANS RELEASING

It's hard for us to let go of our problems. It's difficult to admit we can't solve them ourselves and need help. We flounder and try everything we can think of, but nothing seems to work. What are we overlooking? Maybe if we tried a little harder we'd discover the answer. But there comes a time when the solution is beyond us and we have to turn else-where to find it.

One of the most important lessons I've learned from the Lord is to release my concerns to Him . No matter how long I struggle with them, I'm not going to solve them. So I turn to the One who can. Many talk about letting go and letting God, but how often do they actually do it? It makes such a difference in your life when you do.

My husband, Hank, and I are the founders of As One Ministries, Inc. We're one with each other and one with the Lord. We give Christian seminars to couples, singles and ministers. Several years ago, a univer-sity heard about us and wanted to do a study about our ministry. When they completed their project, they strongly suggested that we convert to a not-for-profit corporation. We fit all the parameters for this kind of business.

Both of us had reservations about doing so. We weren't certain this was the right direction to go, but after much prayer we applied for it. A mountain of red tape was involved plus all the paper work. We hired a lawyer to set up the articles of incorporation and work out some of the other details. The process dragged on for months, from the first of the year to late in the fall. As a result, my husband wasn't sleeping well and I wondered why we were going through all this. At this point, we were ready to forget the whole thing and go back to the way things were.

One morning during our prayer time, we told the Lord we had just about had it. We didn't care if we got the non profit designation or not. If we did, fine. If not, that was all right too. Whatever He wanted was all that mattered. Both of us completely released this concern and put it in His hands. As soon as we did, He answered, "Finally! Now I can get to work." What a big relief that was. A huge weight had fallen off our shoulders. We decided to take a break and glanced at the clock. It was 10 a.m.

That afternoon we got a call from our lawyer who had been out of state. After the initial small talk, he asked my husband if we had heard anything from Atlanta where they were considering our request. "No," he replied. Our lawyer said he had been thinking about it while he was away and wondered why it was taking so long. He decided to call the person who was handling things. He said he got right through to her. This was a bit unusual as his calls were always passed from one person to another before finally reaching her. She told him it was strange that he should call right at that moment as she was just signing her name to our request. We had been approved!

My husband was getting excited by now. "Do you happen to remember what time it was when you called? " Yes, about ten o'clock this morning, our lawyer answered. That was the exact time we had released our concern to the Lord. When we let go and put the situation into the Lord's hands, He went to work just as He said He would. You may consider this a mere coincidence. We don't. We've seen too many things like this happen to dismiss them.

If I'm going to rest in the Lord, that means releasing my concerns to Him. In doing so, there are several steps I usually take.

First, I admit I can't do it. For many of us, that's a big step. When I have to ask for help, that means I'm no longer in control. The other person is. I come to him for advice. I look to him for the answer.

Then I release the problem to the Lord. I let go of entirely - every part of it. I put it out of my mind. But sometimes I forget and find myself taking the problem back and mulling over the possibilities. That's easy to do and I have to remind myself the Lord can handle it very nicely without my help. So if I start thinking about it again, I put it right back in His hands. *As often as it takes.*

I believe He will solve it. Not only can He do it, but I believe He will. Faith is vitally important. Jesus asked the blind men, "Do you believe that I am able to do this? "Yes, Lord," they replied. Then he touched their eyes and said, "According to your faith will it be done to you," and their sight was restored.[1] They saw His mighty power at work.

---

[1] Matthew 9:28-30a

I rest in Him. There isn't any stress or strain on my part because He's the One doing the work. If there is, then I'm not resting in Him. He's a far better problem solver than I am. I don't tell Him what to do or how to do it. I know He wants His best for this situation and will bring it about if I get out of His way. It doesn't matter what He does or how He does it, I know it's right. He's the Lord Almighty, the omniscient One who has all the answers. Nothing is too difficult for Him.

Then I eagerly wait to see what He's going to do. It's exciting to see Him at work. How will He solve this dilemma? His ways are much different than ours. They're better. And they work! "For my thoughts are not your thoughts, neither are your ways my ways," declares the Lord. "As the heavens are higher than the earth, so are my ways higher than your ways and my thoughts than your thoughts." [2]

I thank Him. I not only thank Him when He answers my concerns, I also thank Him before He does a thing. I take hold of the answer now, when I release it to Him. "Therefore I tell you, whatever you ask for in prayer, believe that you have received it, and it will be yours." [3]

Our business is in our home so we never actually get away from it. The Lord has taught us to take short rest breaks with Him throughout the day. Whenever we get bogged down, we stop and "Take 5". We're revived and go back to work with renewed energy. It's like a mini vacation from stress and all the things vying for our attention.

You may want to try it too. It doesn't matter when you take these rest breaks, or where. The Lord is always available. And it doesn't make any difference how long or short they are. Use whatever time you have. Just make sure you take long enough to derive the benefits.

To begin with, lay aside whatever you've been doing. If you're working on a project, put it on the shelf. You can pick it up later. If you like, set the clock for fifteen or twenty minutes. It seems to take that long to unwind and get your mind focused on the Lord instead of what's going on around you. This is a time to just be with Him and appreciate Him. You're concentrating on *now,* not what's going to happen or what already has. If extraneous thoughts flit through your mind, lay them

---

[2] Isaiah 55:8-9
[3] Mark 11:24

aside and come back to them later when your break is over. If they persist, write them down, then forget about them for the present. Often we rush through each day. It's good to slow down for a while. We're not just resting our bodies, but our minds and hearts as well. Regular respites are good for all of us. This is the day the Lord has given us. Enjoy it.

It's interesting to note how often the solution to a project we've been working on comes to mind during these times when we aren't thinking about it. The Lord supplies the answer without our even asking. We're more open to Him not only during our break times, but throughout the rest of the day as well. And when we come to Him several times each day, our concerns don't pile up because we remember to release them to Him one by one.

To Think About:

Do you take your concerns to the Lord every day?

What are the benefits when you do?

What happens when you don't?

Prayer

Father, why is it so hard to let go and let You? Help me to release my concerns to You every day so they don't pile up and weigh me down. Sometimes I forget to do that. I try to handle them myself while You are standing by, ready to help. Thank you for always being there. I pray in the name of Jesus who intercedes for me.

CHAPTER 14

I WILL NEVER BE SHAKEN

I have set the Lord always before me.
Because he is at my right hand,
I will not be shaken.

Psalm 16:8

I WILL NEVER BE SHAKEN

What does it take to shake you up? Do the little zingers that come your way zap you? Someone hurts your feelings. Her words sting yet she's surprised you're upset about it. And just when you're ready to leave work, the boss asks you to type a report at the last minute. He's known about this report all day, but just got around to asking you to do it. You have plans right after work. Talk about frustration! A friend doesn't do what he promised. You feel let down. You trusted him.

You may be able to handle the small things, but the big ones are another story. It takes something truly momentous to rattle you. Like the possibility of losing your job. What would you do? Rumors are flying about a merger. Or what about the lingering pain you have in your leg that won't go away and you wonder if it's something serious. Maybe you should go to a doctor and find out what's wrong. Eventually. You're not sure you want to know. You've been dating someone for over a year and you still don't know where this relationship is headed. Nothing is ever said about it. You know how you feel about him, but how does he feel about you? You're beginning to get seriously interested, but is he? You're afraid to push the matter. You might scare him off and you don't want to do that. What are you supposed to do? What can you do?

For some of us, fear of the unknown devastates us and we come unglued. We like to have everything carefully planned out. We're good at that. That's one of our strengths. Flexibility is not our strong point. We want to know what's going to happen and when so we can prepare for it. We don't like to be confronted with the unexpected. But life is like that. The unexpected hits us out of the blue.

Where does your stress come from? More importantly, what can you do about it? Most of us have situations that can cause a great deal of stress in our lives. Some we can eliminate, but others we can't. We have to live with them. Even if we can't get rid of the cause, we can determine how to handle the stress involved. Ignoring it isn't the answer. Neither is being completely engulfed by it. There is a way that works, however.

Stress isn't something new. It's been around for a long, long time. The psalmist knew about stress and how to keep it from getting the better of him. I have set the Lord always before me.[1] That's a great place to start.

---

[1] Psalm 16:8a

Getting your focus on the Lord and keeping it there. He didn't say now and then or occasionally. He said always, as a way of life. He made it a habit. Something he did everyday.

You may be thinking: "That may have been be easy for him to do. Life was simpler then. How can I possibly keep my mind continually on the Lord with all I have to do? If I try to keep my mind on Him, everything else will suffer." Not necessarily.

Many of us try to handle the tough times ourselves. We don't want to admit we need help. But when we hit rock bottom, we may confide in a trusted ally and friend. It helps to talk things over with someone. There's something even better than that. Turn to the One who knows you better than anyone else. He knows exactly how you feel and what you're going through. He loves you as no one else can or ever will. He is always there for you. He wants you to come to Him with anything and everything. He will comfort, console and guide you. He has a solution for every problem, a way through every dilemma.

What happens when you turn to Him with your troubles and concerns? Because he is at my right hand, I will never be shaken.[2] Bad things may happen to us, but they won't shake us to the core. Hand in hand with Him, we will still be standing and come through them, no matter what they are.

The closer I get to the Lord, the more excited I am about what I have in Him. Listen to this: The righteous cry out, and the Lord hears them; he delivers them from all their troubles.[3] Or this: The Lord is close to the broken hearted and saves those who are crushed in spirit. [4] He means what He says. He backs up His Word by what He has already done. Many times I've said, "Lord I just can't do this." His reply? "I know you can't, but I can. Together we will."

When we're afraid of what might happen, He says, "Never will I leave you; never will I forsake you." [5] "I will be with you. I will see you through this." Can you trust Him? Can you count on Him to come through for you? Yes. He keeps His promises. When others don't, He does.

---

[2] Psalm 16:8
[3] Psalm 34:17
[4] Psalm 34:18
[5] Hebrews 13:5

I know what it is to have Him there when you need Him. When I was facing surgery , I didn't know what lay ahead for me. But one thing I did know. He said He would be with me and I knew He would. And He was. I am convinced that whatever my future holds, He will be there; so there's nothing to fear.

Not only does the psalmist say he will never be shaken, he goes on to say, Therefore my heart is glad and my tongue rejoices; [6]... He doesn't say he's wringing his hands and worrying himself to death. He says he is rejoicing. Can you imagine being in the middle of a tremendous problem and being glad and rejoicing? Not afterward when it's solved, but right in the middle of the adversities knowing that the Lord will come through for you? Being certain that whatever troubles comes along, now or later, He will be there and take you through them. The writer is rejoicing because he has found the answer to all of his problems ...past, present and future... *in the Lord.*

When our minds are focused on the Lord Almighty, then the concerns don't seem so immense after all. The Lord brings them down to size. The Wonderful Counselor is the best counselor of all. He has the solution to every problem there ever was or ever will be. What an awesome God we have!

Then David says, "my body also will rest secure."[7] Do you have trouble sleeping when stress hits you? Sometimes it seems as if your whole life is full of it. You toss and turn all night. Instead of feeling refreshed the next morning, you feel worse than you did the night before. *You took the problem to bed with you and you got up with it.* Next time, release every part of it to the Lord. As long as you hold on to the problem and try to fix it yourself, you hinder Him. He doesn't need your help. He's fully capable to doing it Himself.

The fear of the Lord leads to life: Then one rests content untouched by trouble.[8] Does this mean we'll never have any troubles? No. Problems will come our way. Scripture says: A righteous man may have many troubles. It also says: but the Lord delivers him from them all;[9] *The zingers won't zap us, dilemmas won't defeat us, circumstances won't crush us when we rest secure in Him.*

---

[6] Psalm 16:9
[7] Psalm 16:9
[8] Proverbs 19:23
[9] Psalm 34:19

Things To Think About:

Do you have much stress?

Do you believe God loves you and wants to be involved in every part of your life?

Are you willing to bring your concerns to Him?

Will you take the first step and come to Him now?

Please pray with me:

Father, You tell us to cast all our worries and anxieties on You because You care for us. Right now I an very concerned about:

_____

_____

_____

(Fill in the blanks.)

I give You these concerns of mine. You can handle them far better than I. Thank you for hearing this prayer and answering. I come to You in the name of Jesus, the Wonderful Counselor.

CHAPTER 15

COMING HOME

In my Father's house are many rooms;
if it were not so, I would have told you.
I am going there to prepare a place for you.

John 14:2

COMING HOME

Home. What memories that brings to mind. *Home is where the heart is.* Nothing else can take its place. It doesn't matter if it's big or small, a mansion or a shack. Home is filled with the people we love. We want to be with family, especially on the holidays. One of our sons who is single says Christmas is just like any other day unless he gets to come home. That's what makes it special.

This week I listened to a talk show host interview people about their harrowing experiences in going home for the holidays. Some had cars that broke down on the highway. Others faced bad weather and impassible snow drifts. Delayed flights temporarily stranded a few. Those who called in said they were determined to get home. It was that important to them. They may have been a few hours late but they made it and appreciated being home even more.

Jesus must have longed to go home to His Father. He knew what awaited Him there. For the joy ahead of Him, He endured the agony of the cross. He was gone thirty-three years. That's a long time to be away. Can you imagine the tremendous welcome Jesus received when He went home again? What jubilation there must have been. All heaven celebrated His return and victory over the evil one.

As Christians, we also have a yearning to go home. Back to our roots. The psalmist says: For you created my inmost being; you knit me together in my mother's womb...your eyes saw my unformed body. All the days ordained for me were written in your book before one of them came to be.[1] We began with our Father and we will come home to Him again at the end. In the meantime, we're on quite a journey. For some of us, it's a very brief trip. For others, a long, arduous one. The end of life's journey returns to where it all started...with Him.

Scripture says our life here on earth is but a breath. Compared to eternity, it's over so quickly. Here one day and gone the next. Peter refers to us as aliens and strangers in the world. Jesus said we are to be in the world, but not of it. We're not part of it's value system.

---

[1] Psalm 139:13,16

Instead, we are members of the family of God. Because of the precious blood of His Son, we are adopted into the Father's family. Heirs of God and fellow heirs with Christ. There's no greater family to be a part of! What a rich heritage we have. We have an identity, a family name, a sense of belonging. Paul wrote in Ephesians: ..."I kneel before the Father, from whom his whole family in heaven and on earth derives its name." [2]

What an amazing Heavenly Father we have. He loves us with an unconditional love, not for what we've done but simply because we are His. Our self-worth depends on Him. It's not who we are, but rather *whose* we are. His. We live because of Him. Even with all the children He has, He still knows each of us by name.

There's a purpose for our life. We were created by Him and for Him. All our needs are met. He nurtures and teaches us the Truth that sets us free. Our talents and abilities come from Him and He encourages us to use them to the fullest. He is our security, our refuge , our solid rock. We can count on Him because He never changes.

As His children, the greatest compliment anyone can give us is, "You remind me of your father. I see him in you. There's quite a family resemblance"

Our Father's family is a diverse one, drawn together by His Son. Jesus makes us one. We're all different, yet there is unity . He's the one who holds the family together. There's no need for rivalry or competition. He has more than enough love to go around. In His house, there's always room for one more.

Is it any wonder we look forward to a big family reunion - one made in heaven? We'll see our brothers and sisters in Christ who are already there. They've gone home ahead of us. Will we recognize them after all these years? Will they still remember us? We'll have a lifetime of things to catch up on and forever to do it. We're not just coming home for the holidays. We're coming home for all eternity.

As if that weren't enough, we'll even receive new bodies when we get to heaven. I'm ready for that. No more aches and pains, diets or

---

[2] Ephesians 3:14-15

exercises. This world isn't our home. It's only a temporary stopover. But our citizenship is in heaven. And we eagerly await a Savior from there, the Lord Jesus Christ, who, by the power that enables him to bring everything under his control, will transform our lowly bodies so that they will be like his glorious body.[3]

We aren't the only ones excited about this homecoming. Our Father is too. Jesus told His disciples: "In my Father's house are many rooms; if it were not so, I would have told you. I am going there to prepare a place for you. And if I go and prepare a place for you, I will come back and take you to be with me that you also may be where I am." [4]

As I pondered this, I thought about all the preparations I make for our children when they come home. Their rooms are ready. Favorite foods are prepared. But the most important thing is just being together. These are special times when we enjoy one another.

Our Heavenly Father is preparing for our coming home too. He has a place just for us. He eagerly awaits us with open arms. Precious in the sight of the Lord is the death of his saints.[5] That includes you and me. We don't know the exact time of our arrival, but He does. He's the one who calls us home. He has it all planned out and He'll let us know when the time has come. There's great anticipation and excitement on His part as well as ours.

I can almost hear Him say: "It won't be long distance anymore. We'll be together again. Now you will see Me face to face. No more tears, no more sorrows. The storms of life are over. You'll find love and joy and peace here with Me."

"I've been preparing a room especially for you. I know exactly what you need and what pleases you. Remember, I know everything about you and I want my very best for you. Being with me is far better than anything you had on earth. I love you and I want you to be with Me forever."

---

[3] Philippians 3:20
[4] John 14:2-3
[5] Psalm 116:15

"Because of my Son, you can come home again. He made it all possible. *He paid your way.* He paid for it with His life and He was pleased to do so. In Him is forgiveness and reconciliation. Whatever differences we may have had over the years are all gone...washed away by His blood."

"I knew from the very beginning who would come back to me and who would not. Some choose to stay away. My heart grieves for them, but it's filled with joy for those of you who do come back. Welcome home, my child. I've been looking forward to your return. We've kept in touch through the years, but there's nothing like being here."

Do you know what else is great about being home? We don't have to pretend to be something we aren't. We can just be ourselves. Our Father already knows what we're like. And He loves us the way we are.

No matter how enjoyable this life has been, it's good to go back home. Are you ready? Do you look forward to the big trip? Are there any preparations you need to make? It's time to get your life in order and tie up all the loose ends here. By the way, you don't have to worry about luggage. You won't need it. All you need is you. You came into this world with nothing and you won't carry anything out of it either. Take a good look around before you leave. You won't be coming this way again. Yours is a one way ticket to paradise.

To Think About:

Do you ever wonder what heaven is like?

Are you looking forward to going there to be with your Father?

Is your house in order? Are you ready to come home when He calls?

Prayer

Father, thank you for this life You've given me. Thank you even more so for the privilege of spending eternity with You. Heaven must be an awesome place because You are there. I look forward to seeing You in all Your splendor and glory. How grateful I am to be Your child who is coming home. In the meantime, help me to live a fruitful, fulfilled life here on earth - one that brings You glory.

CHAPTER 16

IF REST IS SO GREAT, WHY DON'T WE?

But the message they heard was of no value to them, because those who heard did not combine it with faith.

Hebrews 4:2

IF REST IS SO GREAT, WHY DON'T WE?

A wonderful rest awaits believers. It is the ultimate rest and the final one. We who are Christ's eagerly look forward to it. Jesus said to Nicodemus: "For God so loved the world that he gave his one and only Son that whoever believes in him shall not perish but have eternal life. For God did not send his Son into the world to condemn the world, but to save the world through him. Whoever believes in him is not condemned, but whoever does not believe stands condemned already because he has not believed in the name of God's one and only Son.[1] We enter this rest through faith in Jesus Christ.

Why are there so many who won't accept this indescribable gift from God? They don't believe it. They prefer a lie instead of the Truth. The Gospel is often watered down, explained away and replaced with alternative routes to heaven. But substitutes don't work. They lead to a far different place, a place where no one would want to go.

Hebrews tells us: Therefore since the promise of entering his rest still stands, let us be careful that none of you be found to have fallen short of it. For we also have had the gospel preached to us, just as they did; but the message they heard was of no value to them, because those who heard did not combine it with faith. Now we who have believed enter that rest,[2]...

For it is by grace you have been saved, through faith - and this not from yourselves, it is the gift of God - not by works, so that no one can boast.[3] Because of His great mercy, God loved us into His Kingdom of Heaven. That's the only way we can enter His eternal rest.

Disobedience is another reason for rejecting God's offer. There are some who refuse to obey Him. They want to do what they want to do rather than what God desires. And to whom did God swear that they would never enter his rest if not to those who disobeyed?[4] God called His people stubborn, obstinate and stiff-necked because they were always going astray. They wouldn't obey Him. Could He say the same thing today?

---

[1] John 3:16-18
[2] Hebrews 4:1-3
[3] Ephesians 2:8-9
[4] Hebrews 3:18

Sometimes an *arrogant attitude* gets in the way. "I don't need God. I can get along quite well without Him. I don't want anyone telling me what to do, even if it's God." I want to be in control of my life. Christians have been called 'losers' because they choose to rely on the Almighty One. How foolish to do otherwise.

Fear is another possibility. "What will I have to give up? I have my rights, don't I? I've worked too hard for them, I don't want to lose them"

Procrastination can be a stumbling block. "I just don't know. I've thought about it, but I can't make up my mind. Maybe I will someday, but not now." They don't realize that later may be too late.

Ignorance is another. Some don't know what they can have. They aren't aware of what they're missing. Not only do they know very little about heaven, they know even less about hell. They're not sure either one exists. Maybe this is all there is.

But we don't have to wait for heaven in order to rest, we can also rest in the Lord while we're still here on earth. And God blessed the seventh day and made it holy, because on it he rested from all the work of creating that he had done.[5] Creation was completed and He commemorated it. He set aside a day of rest for Himself and His people. This would keep their hearts and minds on Him. In the commandments given to Moses the people were told: "Remember the Sabbath day by keeping it holy. Six days you shall labor and do all your work, but the seventh day is a Sabbath to the Lord your God. On it you shall not do any work, neither you, nor your son or daughter, nor your manservant or maidservant, nor your animals, nor the alien within your gates."[6] This was the Lord's day. A time of worship and fellowship when their hearts turned to Him.

We also need a time of rest with the Lord today. As Christians, we set aside the first day of each week to assemble together and worship Him. We take time off in our busy lives to rest in Him.

But rest with Him is available to us every day, not just once a week. It's there for the taking. How many of us do that? What keeps us from it?

---

[5] Genesis 2:3
[6] Exodus 20:8-10a

What hinders us from coming to the Lord daily? He certainly wants this for us. And it's for our own good.

Just as some reject God's eternal rest, they also reject His rest for them here on earth. They don't think they need it. Many of us are very independent individuals. We've been trained to do, do, do. We don't feel comfortable when we don't. Our work ethic is such that we have to do it. It gives us a sense of accomplishment. Instead of leaning on God, we rely on ourselves. We want to be in charge of our lives. We don't want to yield to someone else. If you admit you need help, the one who helps you will be in control. We don't want to be in that subservient position.

Others don't know they can live this way. They think God is far too busy to bother with them on an individual basis. Even if they concede there might be something to it, they are resistant to rest. They don't like change. They're comfortable where they are. It may not be all they'd like, but they prefer the familiar to the unknown.

Some are inundated with all they have to do. They're in over their heads. They are deluged not only with their jobs but also a flood of activities in their lives. Mention rest to them and they answer: "I'm so busy I don't have time to rest. I'll never get it all done as it is. There's too much to do." Satan likes that attitude. It gives him an inroad into their lives. He tries to keep them so busy there's no time left for God. They fail to realize if they don't take time out to rest, burn out isn't far behind.

Whatever the reason, many miss God's best for them. He wants us to rest in Him. We admire Martha for her diligence, but criticize Mary for her lack of it. And yet Jesus said Mary had chosen what is better. I wonder what He would say to us today?

What would it take to convince you to rest in Him? To live this way of life? Are you willing to entrust your life to the One who created you? He alone knows all that it can be. Only He can bring about His best for you. He offers you this rest, but He doesn't make you take it. The choice is yours. Choose life.

To Think About:

What hinders you from resting in the Lord?

Is it worth it?

Prayer

Father, I pray for those who can't make up their minds
about You. Open their hearts to see what they can have
in You. You offer them life - both an abundant one here
on earth and an eternal one in heaven. Thank you for
Jesus who gave us both. We pray this in His name.

ABOUT THE AUTHOR

Mary Ann Kiszla is a writer and speaker who shows what a difference Jesus Christ makes in our lives. She and her husband, Hank, also give Christian seminars for couples, singles and ministers. They are the founders of As One Ministries. A wife, mother and grandmother, Mary Ann is a graduate of DePauw University.

Her other books include *IN HIS HANDS* as well as *AND THE WINNER IS,* a look at spiritual warfare.

Notes

Notes

Notes